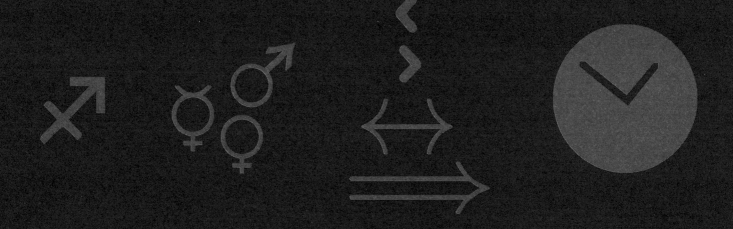

"First we shape the tools, then the tools shape us."

—Marshall McLuhan

THE HISTORY OF
INFORMATION

Written and illustrated by Chris Haughton.

Additional text and research by Loonie Park.

Author & Illustrator Chris Haughton
Additional Text and Research Loonie Park
Consultants Sarosh Arif, Paul Duguid,
and Philip Parker

Senior Acquisitions Editor James Mitchem
Senior Art Editor Charlotte Milner
Editor Becca Arlington
US Senior Editor Shannon Beatty
Designer Eleanor Bates
Design Assistance Sif Nørskov, Anna Pond
Managing Art Editor Diane Peyton Jones
Production Editor Dragana Puvacic
Production Controller John Casey
Picture Research Taiyaba Khatoon,
Samrajkumar S, Rituraj Singh
Jacket Coordinator Elin Woosnam
Art Director Mabel Chan

First American Edition, 2024
Published in the United States by DK Publishing,
a division of Penguin Random House LLC
1745 Broadway, 20th Floor, New York, NY 10019

A catalog record for this book
is available from the Library of Congress.
ISBN: 978-0-7440-9191-5

DK books are available at special discounts
when purchased in bulk for sales promotions,
premiums, fund-raising, or educational use.
For details, contact: DK Publishing Special
Markets,
1745 Broadway, 20th Floor, New York, NY 10019
SpecialSales@dk.com

Printed and bound in China

www.dk.com

CONTENTS

Introduction

This book is dedicated to the memory of Geoff Nunberg.
(1945–2020)

THE HISTORY OF
INFORMATION

Written and illustrated by Chris Haughton.

Additional text and research by Loonie Park.

This book is inspired by the 'History of Information' course created at the
University of California, Berkeley by Paul Duguid and Geoff Nunberg.

What happened to humans?

Until only a few thousand years ago, humans lived in tiny groups and had a difficult, fragile existence. We made only simple stone tools, and in many ways were not very different from any other animal species on Earth. However, today our species dominates the globe and our technologies have transformed the world. How did this happen? How did such an extraordinary change come about?

That is the subject of this book.

We like to tell ourselves the reason we are different from other animals is because we are more intelligent. Maybe there is some truth in this, but most of humanity's most dramatic innovations happened in the last few hundred years, or even the last few decades. We couldn't say that as a species we have become more intelligent in such a short space of time. So what could be causing such a dramatic acceleration in progress?

In this book, we will make the case for a different explanation for our achievements: information.

The sharing of information is nothing new in the natural world. Almost every living species communicates in some way. Plants and bacteria communicate with chemical signals, and animals use combinations of calls, gestures, and scents. Some species need years to teach their young the skills they need to survive. But humans took this and did something more. We found a means of sharing and storing information so that more of it can be passed to the next generation than is lost. In this way, it could accumulate. This was our species' great breakthrough.

Once this process of information accumulation began, it continued like a snowball rolling downhill. Technology built on technology, and each one increased the pace. There have been periods in our early history where little changed, and there may even have been resets. But eventually, our collective gathering and sharing of knowledge led to better and better problem-solving, and progress gained an unstoppable hold—allowing us to create the remarkable complex human world in which we find ourselves today.

How did it all begin? It began with a code. A code with an almost magical quality. A code that allows one brain's thoughts to be sent to another brain so accurately that the other has the very same thought.

Estimated world population: 2 million

Small groups of hunter-gatherers. No humans yet in the Americas.
No large settlements. No villages.

LANGUAGE

"Language is mankind's greatest invention—
except, of course, that it was never invented."

–Guy Deutscher

Language and the brain

How does the brain process language? How does it take these magical strings of sounds and convert them into thoughts? The process can be broken into two stages. First the brain needs to recognize distinctive sounds and convert them into words. Then these words are joined together into sequences. Through these sequences of words, our brains create meaning.

Sounds become words

From birth, we listen intently for different sounds made by the shape of the mouth, and by 18 months we are familiar with all the sounds of our language. From this, we learn that these sounds are pieced together to form words; the simplest units of meaning.

Memory

Humans have a mind-boggling capacity for words. The average adult knows the meaning of an estimated 40,000 words. This means that every child must learn a new word, on average, every three waking hours from the ages of one to eighteen.

Song

Speech and musicality are related. The repetitive 'sing-song' sounds adults make to infants help babies listen to the rhythms and sounds of speech. This is known as baby talk, or infant-directed speech.

Language without sound

Sign language, used by deaf or hard of hearing people, is just as articulate as spoken language.

The world's most universal word is 'mama.' It, or a variation of it, is the word for mother in almost every language, and is often a child's first word.

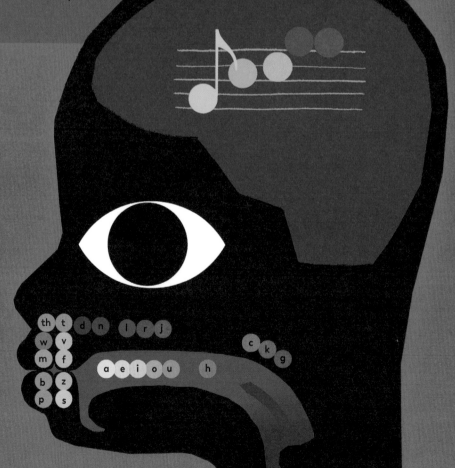

Noam Chomsky   **Nim Chimpsky**

Universal grammar

The linguist Noam Chomsky believes that although humans speak different languages, there is a common structure. He calls this structure 'universal grammar.' In the 1970s, linguists tested this by trying to train chimpanzees to use sign language. A baby chimp was taken into a home and raised alongside young children. He was named Nim Chimpsky. Nim was taught hundreds of signs. Although he seemed to understand and communicate with these words, he was unable to combine words together to form complex sentences like we do. He made three and four word sentences such as 'Banana me eat', 'More eat Nim', and 'Tickle me Nim play,' but seemed unable to understand any of our grammar. However, tests like this are controversial. Aside from ethical concerns, it seems unfair to expect a chimp to learn human systems of communication; after all—humans cannot understand chimpanzee communication.

Sentence

Verb phrase

Noun phrase

Noun phrase

the man hit the rock

Words become sentences

Words combine to form sentences. These units of meaning are strung together to form thoughts. The word order is important—words need to be combined using special rules in order to be understood. All human languages follow similar patterns. Sentence construction is crucial to their meaning.

Grammar

Without grammar, a sentence could have a number of different meanings. The words 'MAN HIT ROCK' can mean all sorts of things. Here are just a few:

The man hit the rock.
A rock that has been hit by a man.
The man will hit the rock.
The rock hit the man.
Did the man hit the rock?
The rock that hit the man.

the man hit the rock

When did language begin?

When and how language began are two of the most debated questions in all of science. The problem is we have very little evidence. Scientists can only speculate based on anatomy from human fossils and our early artifacts.

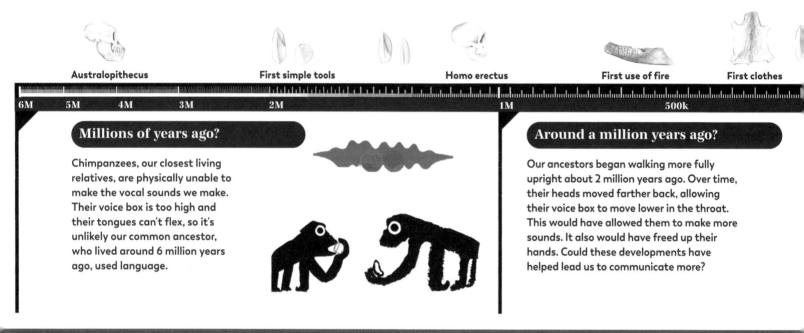

Australopithecus

First simple tools

Homo erectus

First use of fire

First clothes

6M 5M 4M 3M 2M 1M 500k

Millions of years ago?

Chimpanzees, our closest living relatives, are physically unable to make the vocal sounds we make. Their voice box is too high and their tongues can't flex, so it's unlikely our common ancestor, who lived around 6 million years ago, used language.

Around a million years ago?

Our ancestors began walking more fully upright about 2 million years ago. Over time, their heads moved farther back, allowing their voice box to move lower in the throat. This would have allowed them to make more sounds. It also would have freed up their hands. Could these developments have helped lead us to communicate more?

Life before writing

We know very little about the times before writing, but we can try to understand how people might have lived by studying the oral cultures that exist today. Some people today live in remote tribal communities without any writing. These present-day oral cultures may have traits in common with the historic oral cultures of the past.

In traditional societies the elderly are revered and respected. In many societies they are even worshipped.

Elders

Since nothing could be written down or recorded, the only way to preserve important history and knowledge was by memory. Elders in the community had more memories and experiences, so they were often the most reliable source of a people's knowledge and history.

How did language begin?

Nobody really knows. However, for a language to begin there needs to be some amount of trust. In all communication – animal and human – there are elements of information and elements of misinformation. If misinformation outweighed the good, there would be no incentive to evolve complex communication. For a complex language to have formed, there must first have been some level of trust within human society.

Our ancestors are known to have taken care of one another for at least hundreds of thousands of years. We have many examples of this, but one famous example is a skeleton of a neanderthal in a cave in Iraq that dates back around 40,000 years. This man would have been completely crippled by arthritis. But he survived with this severe condition for many years, suggesting he was being cared for by others.

Homo sapiens

Huge advance in tools

50k

50,000 years ago?

Around 50,000 years ago, quite suddenly, our ancestors began making a huge variety of new tools. Could this explosion of technology have been the result of developing language skills?

Local knowledge

In ancient times, knowledge could only be passed from person to person. Also, people did not travel far, because transportation wasn't easy or safe, so knowledge stayed local, too. Skills and technology such as pottery and basket-weaving traveled slowly, and had identifiable local techniques. Myths and stories often spread following the same paths.

The earliest known pottery is from China. It dates back to around 20,000 years ago.

Studying artifacts is one way we can get some idea of how far and fast technology was spreading.

Ceremonies

Our world today functions on paperwork and documents. But what did people do before writing? To mark and remember an important moment, they gathered many witnesses together to celebrate it and create a collective memory of the event. These are known as ceremonies.

Coronations

Crowning a new leader is one of the most important ceremonies in society. To ensure a successful rule, there should be general agreement among the people to accept the new ruler. For this reason, a coronation is usually the most elaborate ceremony of all.

Coronation ceremony—Benin, West Africa

The Oba of Benin

In Benin, the 'Oba' or leader sits on a throne, holds a scepter, and wears a special headdress called an Adé (crown) and elaborate royal garments. These same ancient symbols of power are used not just in Africa, but all over Europe, Asia, the Americas, and the rest of the world.

Extravagant food, drink, and entertainment are often provided for guests.

Coronation ceremony—London, UK

Coronations are often performed by religious authorities so that the monarch's rule is accepted by the population. The ceremonies often include displays of power such as grand military processions. The British Monarch is both head of the Church of England and of the British Armed Forces.

The larger the crowd of witnesses at a ceremony, the more it is validated.

In ancient Egypt, the many coronation rituals of the Pharaoh were spread out across a whole year of festivities.

Modern ceremonies

Ancient ceremonies, particularly weddings and religious rituals, continue in different forms all over the world today. A traditional Hindu wedding celebration can last for three or more days. The bride and groom wear elaborate clothing, and many religious and traditional rituals are performed.

Many wedding customs in Europe are also very old. The earliest wedding ceremonies took the form of processions from the home of the bride to the home of the groom. This is echoed by the bridal procession down the aisle in Christian celebrations. But wedding rings, and even cakes also pre-date Christianity.

Some modern wedding customs have troubling origins. The tradition of the groomsman is believed to originate from the time of the Germanic Goths. They were there to stop the bride running away or to prevent her family stopping the wedding.

Ceremonial objects

Symbolic objects are often used in ceremonies. It is sometimes customary to exchange rings at a wedding to serve as a reminder of the vows. Likewise, crowns, gowns, and scepters are also used in ceremonies.

The tradition of exchanging rings in western traditions is of very ancient origin, perhaps dating back to ancient Egyptian times, 4,000 years ago.

The art of remembering

Before writing, all information had to be remembered and passed on 'orally,' using only spoken language. Communities who lived in a society without writing are known as 'oral cultures.' Even without writing, they had ways to pass on information through the generations.

Myths

The word 'myth' comes from the Greek word 'mythos', which means 'from the mouth'. Oral tales often have mythological traits that are usually exaggerated and have fantastical details. Characters that are half-human/half-horse, or have snakes for hair are very memorable—and in oral cultures, only the most memorable stories survive to be retold.

The Mahabharata

This ancient Indian poem is almost 2 million words (50x the length of this book) and believed to be the world's longest. It tells the heroic adventures of different gods, along with moral teachings. Its survival over thousands of years through memory and retelling alone shows just how much it was valued.

"Words are invaluable, speak them if you must. Weigh them carefully before you speak them out."

People in ancient societies entertained themselves through poetry, song, and stories. There was, after all, little other entertainment.

Memorization

Human memory is flawed, especially over long time periods, so to help memorize accurately, clever techniques were devised. Ancient India had some of the most sophisticated oral traditions in the world. The Vedic chants use rhythm and rhyme 'pathas' to ensure the words in each verse are accurate. Today, we still use a few similar devices—to remember the months we have a rhyme: "30 days have September, April, June, and November..."

Ways to remember

Rhyme, rhythm, and repetition help us remember wording. You probably can't remember the exact words of even one or two lines from a favourite book, but you can likely repeat many lines word for word from lots of different songs or poems.

The myths still with us today

The myths and stories from the very earliest civilizations are still with us today in all sorts of ways. Here are some myths that have left a mark on western culture.

Sumerian myths

The Sumerians of Mesopotamia (present-day Iraq) worshipped the planets as gods. The days of the week come from the sun, moon, and five visible planets. Venus was very important. They called her 'Inanna,' the god of fertility, love, and beauty—but also of war. She was associated with the eight-pointed star and dove. She, and others, have echoed through the ages. The Babylonians and Persians worshipped her as 'Ishtar,' the Phoenicians as 'Astarte,' the Hindus as 'Durga,' the Greeks as 'Aphrodite,' the Romans as 'Venus,' and the Norse as 'Freya.'

Greek myths

Greek myths, like those in many cultures, feature memorable characters: the one-eyed Cyclops, the Minotaur who was part-human and part-bull, and Gorgons with snakes for hair, who could turn people to stone with their gaze. Also pictured here is Aphrodite with a dove. She was also associated with red roses. These symbols are used today for peace and romantic love.

Norse myths

In English, the days of the week derive from the Norse gods pictured below. Tuesday, Tyr's day, comes from the god 'Tyr,' Wednesday, Woden's day from 'Woden,' Thursday from 'Thor,' and Friday from 'Freya.' Norse myths were kept alive by memory alone until around 1250 CE. Only then were they finally written down.

The Epic of Gilgamesh

This epic poem from Sumer, Mesopotamia, is heavily mythologized, but is thought to be based on a real king who lived around 5,000 years ago. It long pre-dates the Bible, but the two have many similar stories. There is a great flood, a snake that tempts the main characters, and a hero born of a virgin mother.

Old Testament Bible

Abraham, a spiritual leader from the ancient city of Ur, also in Mesopotamia, played a significant role in the Old Testament Bible. His life and teachings were eventually transformed into the stories found in the book of Genesis. These, along with others, were later gathered and written down, resulting in the creation of the Old Testament Bible.

3000 BCE

Estimated world population: 14 million

Humans are living all across the world and have begun farming. Populations are dense in at least four agricultural regions: The Fertile Crescent; Nile River, Egypt; Indus River; and Northern China.

Largest cities: 1. Uruk (40,000), 2. Nagar, 3. Eridu

Large stone structures are found all over the world, sometimes with carvings. Stonehenge is perhaps the most famous. It is aligned toward sunrise on summer solstice and sunset on winter solstice.

DRAWING

"The aim of art is to represent not the outward appearance of things, but their inward significance."

–Aristotle

First marks

Mark making is the crucial first step that led us to drawing. The idea of a mark representing something else is so familiar to us today that we forget what an extraordinary idea it is. In a way, everything in this book follows from this idea.

Foil

Stock

If lenders were not paid back they would be left with nothing more than 'the short end of the stick.'

200,000 BCE

Hand prints

The first known deliberate markings are these hand and footprints found in a cave in present-day China. They were not made by homo sapiens, but by our early ancestors. These particular markings appear to be made by two people, one around 7, and the other around 12 years old. These types of markings became common all over the world. An analysis shows that of all the cave hand paintings, around three quarters appear to be made by women and children.

43,000 BCE

Indexes

The earliest known recording systems are marks notched on a piece of bone, wood, or stone. One stroke represents one, two strokes represent two, and so on. This notched bone from present-day South Africa, known as the Lebombo bone, is an early example of these indexes. It is around 43,000 years old, and analysis reveals that many of its 29 marks were made by different tools, indicating that it was probably notched over time. By around 30,000 BCE, indexes were being used all over the world.

Tally sticks

The tally is an index system where marks were made on a stick which was then split in two. One half was kept by the lender. It was called the 'stock' and is the origin of the word for the stock market. The other half, kept by the borrower, was called the 'foil.' When the borrower returned with the goods they would be 'tallied' (which means the two halves would be matched). Tally sticks were popular in medieval Europe, and were used to show how much money, goods, and tax were owed.

Number systems

Number systems around the world originally came from indexes. Pictured here, top to bottom, are the Mayan numerals, Chinese numerals, Latin numerals, and ancient Indian Brahmi numerals. Our modern western numerals (1,2,3) and the Arabic numerals (١،٢،٣) are derived from Brahmi numerals.

Indexes used today

Latin numerals

Although the Hindu-Arabic numerals (0, 1, 2, 3) have taken over from the Latin numerals as the world's most common number system, Latin numerals are still used in certain situations. In some cases, to emphasize longevity and tradition, they are deemed the only correct usage. For instance, in English, it is deemed incorrect to write 'Queen Elizabeth 2' instead of 'Elizabeth II.'

Prayer beads

Rosary and prayer beads used in many religions today also trace their origins back to index memory devices.

3000 BCE

Quipu

The most advanced system of indexing was used by the Inca Empire. They used a system of knots, or 'quipu', to record stock and sales, census information, and calendars. The Inca are said to be the most advanced civilization to have not invented a proper writing system. They managed to somehow code information in only knots. Sadly, the knowledge of how to decipher of many of these codes was lost after the European invasions, and they can no longer be understood.

First drawings

The concept of drawing is central to the story of information. The Greek word for drawing is 'graph'. Many innovations in this book; photography, telegraph, and graphical interfaces, derive from this concept.

45,000 BCE

Cave art

Cave paintings and drawings began to emerge around 45,000 years ago, and by 30,000 years ago, they were found in human settlements all across the globe. The earliest drawn images are all of animals, it was only later that we drew other humans.

Indonesia
This is the earliest known figurative drawing in the world—a depiction of a wild pig in Sulawesi, Indonesia. It is believed to be at least 45,000 years old.

Australia
Australia has a rich visual culture. Their distinctive rock art is some of the oldest in the world. At one site, Gabarnmung, a series of tunneled caves had been inhabited for 40,000 years. Artwork there dates from 28,000 years ago, and the caves had been continuously used until the 20th century.

4000 BCE

Pottery markings

Ancient Egyptian hieroglyphs seem to have evolved from early markings and drawings made on pottery. Pottery markings and seals also emerged in nearby Sumer and in India around the same time.

The Rainbow Serpent is a creator god in Australian cultures. Images of it can be traced back 8,000 years. This would make it the world's oldest known belief system.

Aboriginal Australians could navigate vast desert regions by reciting 'song lines'—oral chants which acted like maps across the land.

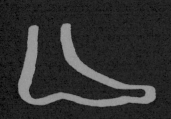

Drawings become concepts

Images are very useful communication tools, but they do have limitations. For instance, it is possible to represent 'man' or 'woman' but it is very difficult to represent 'brother.' Over time, images came to be used for more abstract ideas. For example, ancient Egyptians used an image of a foot to symbolize 'walk,' 'go,' or 'come.'

Icons

Icons are in common use today, and work in the same way as hieroglyphics. An example of this is how an image of a glass is commonly printed on packaging to symbolize 'fragile.' Glasses are associated with fragility, so the image is used on boxes with fragile contents. In this way, images are used for signage, interfaces, and road signs to communicate messages. Religious icons and government seals are still highly respected symbols.

3200 BCE

Hieroglyphs

Ancient Egyptian hieroglyphs, along with Sumerian cuneiform, are the world's earliest symbol systems. Hieroglyphs date back to earlier than 3200 BCE. Some of the most important hieroglyphic signs were believed to hold supernatural qualities.

The evil eye and Christian cross.

The UK Government seal features a crown, and the US seal features an eagle. Both are ancient symbols of power. Different variations of the cross and these government seals can be seen at key moments throughout this book.

Ouroboros

The snake eating its tail was a symbol of rebirth and infinity. Like many hieroglyphic symbols, it evolved in different forms under later civilizations. This symbol was common in Greek and Norse cultures.

Was Scepter

The 'Was' was the Pharaoh's scepter. It symbolized power, not just of the Pharaoh, but of the gods.

Eye of Horus

The all-seeing eye of the god Horus was believed to have protective qualities. It has evolved into similar signs today to ward off the 'evil eye.'

Ankh

The 'Ankh' symbol meant 'life' and especially 'eternal life.' It was revered in many cultures around Egypt. The Christian cross is believed to have been in part inspired by the sign 2000 years later.

Combinations of two or more signs were sometimes used to express abstract ideas. For example, a person and a mountain together was taken to mean 'foreigner,' or an eye and water together meant 'weep.'

The first city

The Sumerian city, Uruk, in present-day Iraq, was the world's first city. By 3000 BCE it was the largest settlement on Earth, with 40,000 people. To manage such a large population an accounting system was needed. But for an accounting system, there first needs to be writing...

First tokens

In around 7000 BCE, Sumerians began using small clay counting tokens called 'calculi' as a way to do accounting. Each differently shaped token represented a type of stock. One represented sheep, another a goat, another a measure of grain, and so on. The three tokens marked with a '+' (pictured above) represent three sheep. They can be seen as not only a precursor to writing, but also to money.

First writing

Around 4000 BCE, tokens were replaced with a system of drawing the token shapes directly onto clay tablets with a stick. Pictured here is the symbol for sheep. Like the token, it also has a '+' sign, but the three dots next to it mean it represents three sheep. This system eventually evolved into a full writing system, called cuneiform.

The other symbols pictured represent beer, barley, ox, and vessel.

First invoices

This image is a recreation of a grain invoice to a brewer from 3200 BCE. The text reads '29,086 measures (of) barley, 37 months, Kushim.' Kushim is mentioned on several tablets. Presumed to be an accounting official, Kushim is believed to be the first named person in history.

Many early innovations came from Sumer, including the plow, the sail, and the wheel.

Trade

Before there was a system of trading, everyone needed to do everything themselves. Many different skills were needed by each individual. A farmer not only had to farm, but also make and repair their own tools. Trading allows people to specialize in particular skills and knowledge.

In Sumer, there was an explosion of specialized trades, such as ceramics, metalworking, and carpentry. Each trade could become more specialized, taking years to master. Trade allows the sum of human knowledge to grow so everyone benefits.

The character for beer can be seen on the left and barley on the right. The dots are the numbers.

First literature

Writing was eventually used for other things besides accounting. Stories were written down for the first time. Around 2100 BCE, *The Epic of Gilgamesh* (p.15), an oral tale, was recorded in writing. It is considered to be the oldest work of literature.

The Sumerian high priests

The Sumerians believed that the supreme rulers of their cities were not kings, but gods. In the middle of each Sumerian city, a pyramid-like structure called a 'ziggurat' was built. A temple was built on top dedicated to the city's god. In Uruk, it was the sky god An and his daughter Inanna (p.15) that were worshipped.

Priests collected offerings on behalf of the gods, using writing to record the items collected for their temple and ensure that everyone paid. The Sumerian word for priest, 'sangar', is also the word for 'accountant.' Sumerian writing became very complex and difficult to learn, and to much of the population, reading and writing may have seemed like an almost supernatural ability.

Today

Many of the units we use today came to us from the ancient Sumerians more than 5000 years ago.

Maths

The Sumerians were expert mathematicians. They discovered how to calculate the area of a triangle and volume of a cube. They used the number 60 instead of 10 as their base in counting. The division of a circle into 360 degrees came to us from Sumer.

360°   Area of triangle   Volume of cube

Astronomy and astrology

The Sumerians made star charts and noted the movements of the planets. There are five planets visible to the naked eye, these five plus the Sun and Moon total seven. To the Sumerians, seven was a sacred number. They created the seven-day week we use today based on the seven heavenly bodies. In English only three of these names remain (Saturn-day, Sun-day and Moon-day), but in many languages, they are still named after the planets. The practice of astrology also dates back to Mesopotamia.

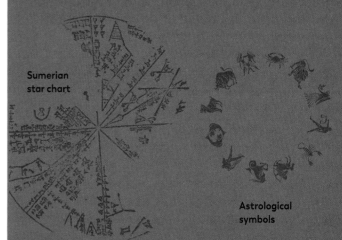

Sumerian star chart

Astrological symbols

The invention of time

The Sumerians also gave us many of our units of time: One minute (60 seconds), one hour (60 minutes), one day (12 hours, plus 12 hours for one night), and one week (7 days).

First writing systems

As writing developed, pictures became more simple so they could be drawn more quickly. Instead of pictures, they became symbols, each with a meaning. This type of writing is called 'ideographic writing', and each symbol represents an idea.

Egypt

3200 BCE

A complex writing system, known as hieroglyphic, evolved in Egypt. It had more than 900 symbols. Later it was adapted into a shorthand version known as 'hieratic' which was used for writing on papyrus, a type of early paper made of reeds.

Crete (Greece)

1800 BCE

Two early scripts have been found on artifacts in Crete. Linear A, above, has not yet been deciphered, but Linear B, to the right, has.

Sumer

3500 BCE

The first writing system originated in Sumer. This script is known as cuneiform, meaning 'wedge-shaped' in Latin.

Indus Valley

2600 BCE

In the Indus Valley, in what is now northwest India and Pakistan, seals were used to indicate ownership. These appear to have evolved into a full writing system. However, the writings are as yet undeciphered.

China

1200 BCE

According to legend, writing in China was invented by the Emperor from his studies of nature, particularly animal and bird footprints.

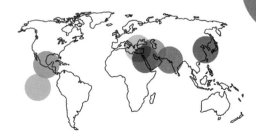

Drawing sounds

A clever way to represent difficult words visually is by breaking the words apart. For example, the English word 'idea' can be represented with a drawing of an eye and a drawing of a deer (eye-deer). This is known as the 'rebus principle'. It was used in many ancient writing systems.

Ideographs used today

We use many ideographs in our day-to-day lives. Logos, play and pause buttons, road signs, musical notes, and mathematical signs, are all examples of ideographs.

Symbolic writing is efficient. For example 'E=MC2' is easier to work with and understand than 'energy is equal to mass multiplied by the speed of light squared'. For this reason, symbols are often used in math.

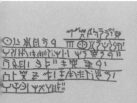

Unknown

Rapa Nui (Easter Island)

Thought to be yet another independent invention of writing, the meanings behind the script found on Easter Island have been lost, and are still undeciphered by scientists.

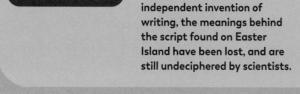

Maya

Writing was independently invented in the Americas by the Maya in Central America. The earliest known Mayan writings were found on a temple in Guatemala. Writing came to be widely used across the region, and books with the script were created from bark paper.

300 BCE

In ancient China, one of the earliest uses for writing was to make prophecies. Characters were carved into animal bones, which were heated in a fire until they cracked. If a crack went through one of the symbols, the divination was interpreted. Many common Chinese characters date back to these origins.

Symbolic writing however, tends to be very complex. Full languages require thousands of characters. Mandarin has around 8,000 characters in common use.

| 1200 BCE | 1100 BCE | 400 BCE | 200 BCE | 200 CE |

Pictured here is the character for horse. Pronounced 'ma', it is also one of the 12 Chinese zodiac signs. Like many characters, its shape has changed by being written and rewritten many times over centuries.

In 1956, the Chinese characters (hanzi) were simplified so that they could be more easily learned. On the left is the traditional Chinese character for horse, and on the right is the simplified character. Traditional characters are used in Hong Kong, while simplified Chinese is used on the mainland.

Drawings become sound

The majority of written languages used today are 'phonographic,' which literally means 'sound drawing.' Reading phonographs is almost like hearing with your eyes.

The alphabet

The alphabet can be traced back to ancient Egyptian hieroglyphics. The Egyptian word for 'ox' was pronounced 'alp,' so the symbol for ox began to be used to describe the sound 'A.' The word for house was 'bet' and so a symbol of a house was used for 'B.' This is where we get the word 'alphabet.'

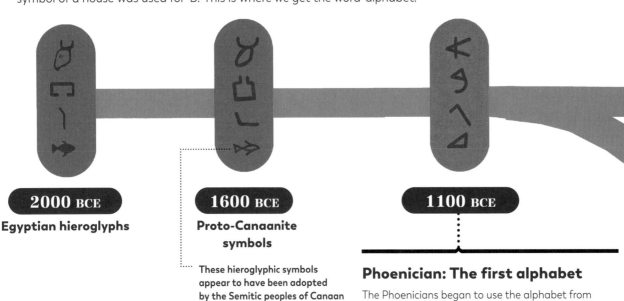

2000 BCE

Egyptian hieroglyphs

1600 BCE

Proto-Canaanite symbols

These hieroglyphic symbols appear to have been adopted by the Semitic peoples of Canaan and the Sinai Desert before being used by the Phoenicians and spreading across the world.

1100 BCE

Phoenician: The first alphabet

The Phoenicians began to use the alphabet from around 1100 BCE. They traded all across the Mediterranean, spreading the alphabet and writing as they went. Their main city was Byblos, in present day Lebanon, which is where we get the word 'Bible.'

The Phoenicians

The Phoenicians were expert shipbuilders. They developed the rounded wooden keels still used today. They also produced all sorts of luxury goods; most famous of all was their purple dye. It was so rare and valuable it became the color of royalty all over the ancient world. The word 'Phoenician' actually means 'purple.'

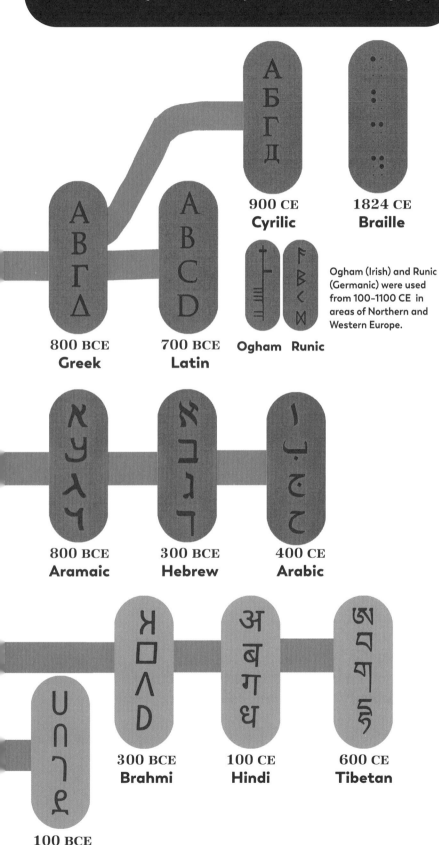

Nonphonetic signs

The '&' symbol evolved from the alphabet back into an ideograph. It began as the letters 'Et,' the Latin for 'and.' Scribes began linking the two letters together from the 1st century CE. While it is pronouced 'and' in English, it is pronouced as 'und', 'y', 'et', 'e', and 'och' in other languages.

900 CE
Cyrilic

1824 CE
Braille

Ogham (Irish) and Runic (Germanic) were used from 100–1100 CE in areas of Northern and Western Europe.

800 BCE
Greek

700 BCE
Latin

Ogham   **Runic**

800 BCE
Aramaic

300 BCE
Hebrew

400 CE
Arabic

300 BCE
Brahmi

100 CE
Hindi

600 CE
Tibetan

100 BCE
Ethiopic

Phonographics today

Almost every script in use today traces back to ancient Egyptian hieroglyphs. The exceptions are Chinese, Japanese, and Korean. Phonic scripts can be categorized into three groups: alphabets, abjads, and abugidas.

Alphabets

The alphabets (shown to the left in orange) are the most widely used. They represent all the sounds of the language, consonants, and vowels.

Abjads

The abjads (shown in pink) represent only consonants, not vowels. The word Islam, for example, is spelled 'slm.' Arabic, Syriac, and Hebrew are still in modern use. They are written from right to left.

Abugidas

The abugidas (shown in blue) spell out syllables rather than individual sounds. The Ge'ez script evolved in Africa and is used to write Ethiopian and Eritrean. Brahmi evolved in northern India and splintered into dozens of scripts as it spread into South India and East Asia. Pictured below are examples from: North India: Bengali and Punjabi; South India: Kanneda and Mayalam; and South East Asia: Burmese and Thai.

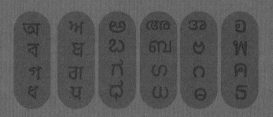

Korean

The Korean Hangul alphabet has no relation to the other alphabets. It was invented in 1443 to replace the Chinese characters which were used at that time in Korea. The Chinese characters take many years to learn, but Hangul is considered the most efficient and phonetic of all the scripts, and its forms reflect the shapes of a mouth. Rather than years, it can be 'learned in a morning' according to its inventor, King Sejong.

1000 BCE

Estimated world population: 50 million

Densely populated regions spread. The first empires begin.

Largest cities: 1. Thebes (120,000), 2. Babylon, 3. Memphis

Using simple bronze tools, set squares, and plumb lines, Egyptians of this time were able to create the precise straight lines and right angles of their monumental architecture.

WRITING

"In the beginning was the Word, and the Word was with God, and the Word was God."

—The Bible, King James Version, John 1:1

Early writing

Around 6,000 years ago, changes were seen in ancient societies. They were becoming male-dominated. It is believed that this is because of the rise of military warrior-states. Writing later began being adopted by states as a tool to rule.

Laws

Before writing, rulers ruled with only spoken commandments. After the invention of writing, many of these commands were written down as laws. This meant the rulers could rule from afar, which allowed states to grow larger. Criminal punishments were often equal to the crime (an eye for an eye, a tooth for a tooth). However, crimes committed against the state or the state religion were severely punished. Even just speaking out against the state, in many cases, could mean a death sentence. Legal systems all over much of the ancient world were based on similar principles.

> "An eye for an eye, a tooth for a tooth."
>
> – Hammurabi

This famous phrase has its origins in the *Code of Hammurabi*. It is one of the first known sets of written laws. Many of its principles found their way into other later codes of law, including the Hebrew Laws (the Torah), and the Bible.

Some of the earliest writings were declarations of greatness and victories.

> "I am important, I am magnificent. With their blood I dyed the mountain red."
>
> – Ashurnasirpal II, King of Assyria

> "I am Ashurbanipal, King of the World, King of Assyria."
>
> – Ashurbanipal, King of Assyria

Early law codes were extremely misogynistic. Women were spoken about in the *Code of Hammurabi* as if they were possessions.

1755–1750 BCE
Code of Hammurabi, Babylon

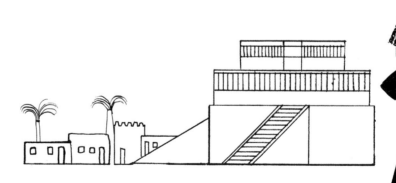

Ashurbanipal was one of the first kings in history who could read and write. He created the world's first library in his palace. As well as boasting of his greatness he also boasted of his learnedness.

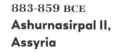

883-859 BCE
Ashurnasirpal II, Assyria

How did society become dominated by men?

The historian Gerda Lerner, and others, believe that in the earliest societies, women and men were considered equals, but these cultures were displaced by the rise of male-dominated warrior states. In Europe and Asia this is believed to have happened around 6,000 years ago, in the so-called 'Kurgan hypothesis'. In almost every society since, women were discouraged from reading and writing. In many societies they were punished if they even attempted to learn. This means that the contributions of women have been almost completely erased from history. Sadly, because of this, much of the rest of this book depicts mostly men. There are exceptions. The Tuareg people of the Sahara are one. In Tuareg culture, it was mainly women who read and write. The woman is the head of the Tuareg household, but men and women are considered equals. As with a handful of other societies around the world, their culture seemed to escaped the grip of these oppressive warrior states.

A Tuareg woman writing in Tifinagh script. Tifinagh dates from 600 BCE

Logic

Drawing and writing changed how we think. Geometry, for example, would be almost impossible without drawing. Writing too, allows us to categorize things in ways we would otherwise find very difficult if we could only use our heads. The ideas of 'deduction' and 'proof' came from early legal systems because guilt needed to be proven. From this, Aristotle developed a system of reasoning called 'logic.' A premise is shown, using deductions, to be either true or false.

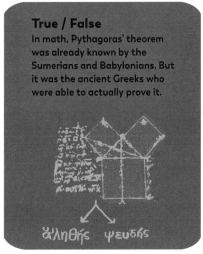

True / False
In math, Pythagoras' theorem was already known by the Sumerians and Babylonians. But it was the ancient Greeks who were able to actually prove it.

ἀληθής   ψευδής

Is writing a good thing?

The philosophers Confucius and Socrates both lived around the time writing began to be widely used, but held different views on it. Confucius is one of the most influential thinkers of all time. He collected writings and spoke about the importance of preserving knowledge for future generations. He lived in a time of terrible wars in ancient China, and argued that if agreed laws were written down and followed by everyone, there could be an end to war.

In ancient Greece, however, Socrates argued that texts cannot contain true knowledge because you can't question them. He worried that memory and the art of questioning would become lost if writing was relied upon. His students, Plato and then Aristotle, eventually warmed to writings and the knowledge they can contain. Aristotle even started a library toward the end of his life.

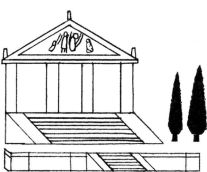

Later, the ancient Greeks began to build great libraries. The library of Alexandria may have held as many as 400,000 scrolls.

551-479 BCE
Confucius
Ancient China

470-399 BCE
Socrates
Ancient Greece

250 BCE
Library of Alexandria

Holy texts

Collections of writings began to be compiled into bodies of knowledge: creation stories, histories, philosophies, guides for living good lives. These became our holy texts, and the great world religions were born.

Sacred scripture

For people who had never been exposed to writing before, the act of reading many hace seemed like a supernatural ability. People who could read and write were looked at in awe, and sometimes even feared. One common use of early writing was for wills and testaments. When these were read aloud, illiterate people would hear the words and thoughts of their dead relative being magically spoken again. Writing in some ways could transcend death, which may be another reason why texts became so revered.

Book of the Dead

1550 BCE

The *Book of the Dead*, or as it was called at the time: *The Book of Emerging Forth into the Light*, was a collection of ancient Egyptian texts, including spells intended to assist a dead person's journey through the underworld. It was often written inside coffins.

Hieroglyphs

Hieroglyphs means 'holy carvings' in Greek. Hieroglyphs were mainly used for sacred purposes by the Pharaohs, priests, and those in authority. The word 'hierarchy' meaning 'holy rule' has a similar root.

In the *Book of the Dead* the heart of the deceased is weighed on a scale against a feather to test if it is 'true of voice'. If the soul is heavier than the feather it will be devoured by the crocodile god Ammit. Thoth, the god of writing, wisdom, and judgement observes.

"I live again and again after death like Ra day by day."

The invention of the book

The format of the book that we know today was developed in ancient Rome around 100 CE. Books were much easier to search and flip through than scrolls. They were also more economical, as text can be written on both sides. The first Christians adopted the book in order to differentiate themselves when they split from Judaism. The spread of the book format is associated with the rise of Christianity. By the year 500 CE books had almost entirely replaced scrolls.

Cosmic dance
The Goddess Kali dances on the body of Shiva. Shiva represents consciousness, and Kali represents time—the ultimate slayer of all things. In Hinduism, cosmic reality is represented by the dance of time (Kali) upon the unchanging pervading consciousness (Shiva).

Rig Veda

1500 BCE

India is home to some of the world's earliest religious writings, but unlike other major religions, Hinduism does not place huge importance on texts. The roots of Hindusim long predate the invention of writing, so oral traditions were favored. Even today, there is a tradition of spiritual gurus rather than relying on holy texts.

"The truth is one, the wise call it by many names."

Hebrew Bible

1000–100 BCE

Judaism is the first of the three Abrahamic religions, which also include Christianity and Islam. The Hebrew Bible is a collection of texts from prophets such as Abraham and Moses. It also includes the *Torah* which means 'The Law.' Traditionally these texts were, and still are, written on a large scroll.

"Love your neighbor as yourself."

Christian Bible

100 CE

The Christian text, the Bible, is in two parts, the Old and New Testaments. The Old Testament contains the Hebrew teachings. The New Testament is based on the teachings of a new prophet, Jesus, whom Christians believe to be the Messiah. It was written in the 1st century.

"Love your enemies and pray for those who persecute you."

The Sutras

500 BCE

Buddhism was the first religion in the world that was spread through writing. It began in Nepal and India, and as it was popular among the literate classes, especially merchants, it spread through trade routes and soon became very popular in areas where there were high levels of trade and literacy, especially East Asia.

"All that we are is the result of what we have thought."

The Qur'an

610 CE

Islam is considered the third Abrahamic faith because Muslims believe in the Prophesy of Abraham, Moses, and Jesus. The Prophet Muhammad is believed to be the final prophet from God, to which the holy Qur'an was revealed, beginning in 610 CE. In 622 CE, Muhammad migrated to Medina, marking the start of the Islamic calendar.

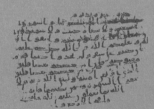

"And do not mix the truth with falsehood or conceal the truth while you know [it]."

Ancient China

For much of history, ancient China was the world's largest empire. Even when the Roman Empire was at its height, the Chinese Empire at the time was larger. Writing was adopted early by the Chinese government and they used it to rule.

Classic texts of Ancient China

A rich culture of calligraphy and ink brush painting has existed in East Asia for millennia. The great calligraphers of China are household names in a similar way to the Renaissance artists of Europe.

The I Ching

1000–750 BCE

Divination text (p57).

The Analects

475–221 BCE

Confucius' famous text was compiled by his followers.

Records of the Grand Historian

110–90 BCE

A mammoth work originally written on bamboo slips. It covers 2,500 years of history and took more than 18 years to write.

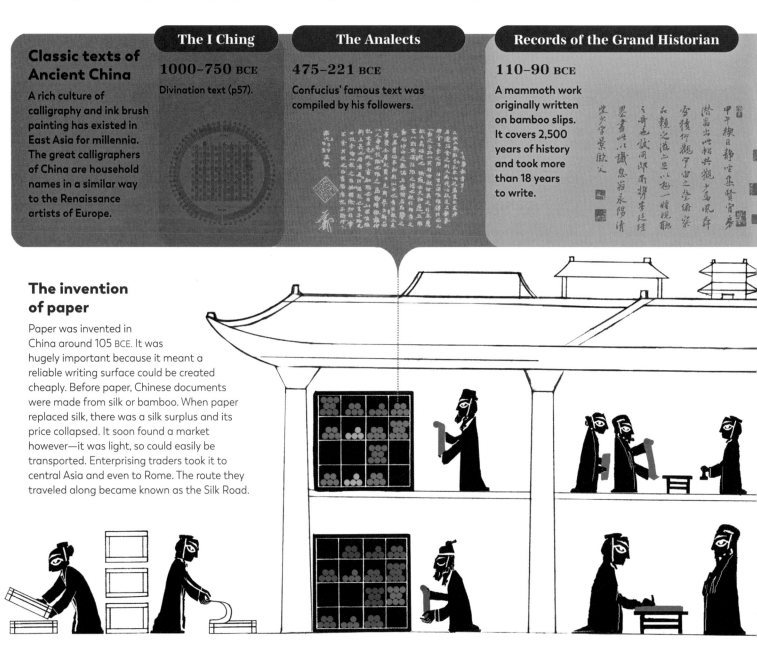

The invention of paper

Paper was invented in China around 105 BCE. It was hugely important because it meant a reliable writing surface could be created cheaply. Before paper, Chinese documents were made from silk or bamboo. When paper replaced silk, there was a silk surplus and its price collapsed. It soon found a market however—it was light, so could easily be transported. Enterprising traders took it to central Asia and even to Rome. The route they traveled along became known as the Silk Road.

Wood or fibre is pulped and laid on a screen.

The screens are dried in the sun.

The dried paper is peeled off the screens.

First libraries

The first libraries began to appear in China around 1600 BCE. By around 220 CE, the Imperial Library was so large it had 10 paper makers tasked with supplying the library with enough paper. It collected China's literature, histories, poetry, and philosophy. Although China was perhaps the most literate society in the world at this time, it is estimated that only around one in five men there could read.

Government bureaucracy

Chinese officials dictated orders for scribes to copy or write. To keep the giant government running, thousands of literate employees were required. Government officials used their own signature stamp, which was registered and used in all documents. This practice continues today.

Authentication

When something is said out loud we know who said it. But how can anyone be sure that a piece of text is written by the person named on it? A system of stamps, signatures, and wax seals have been created to try to ensure authenticity of authors. With intricate details and near identical imprints, stamps are far more difficult to forge than a signature.

The Dunhuang Star Map

700 CE

The world's oldest star atlas.

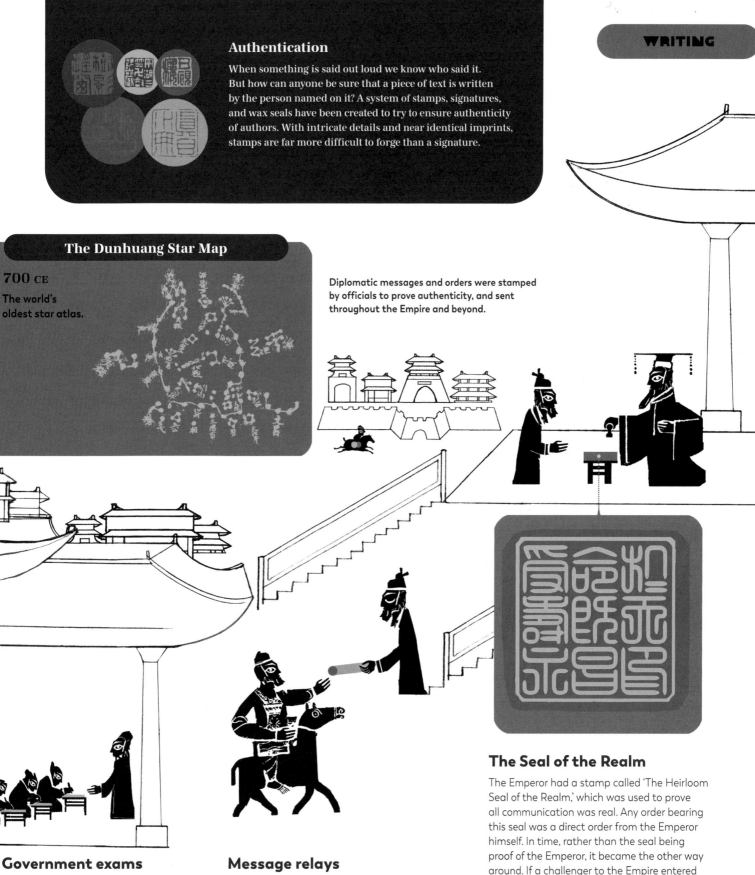

Diplomatic messages and orders were stamped by officials to prove authenticity, and sent throughout the Empire and beyond.

The Seal of the Realm

The Emperor had a stamp called 'The Heirloom Seal of the Realm,' which was used to prove all communication was real. Any order bearing this seal was a direct order from the Emperor himself. In time, rather than the seal being proof of the Emperor, it became the other way around. If a challenger to the Empire entered the palace and took control of the government and the use of the seal, it meant that the government had been overthrown and a new leader had rightfully become Emperor. It was said if anyone was able to seize control of the seal they had received the 'Mandate of Heaven.' In many ways, the seal was not the proof of power—it was the power itself.

Government exams

Around 607 CE, a state-wide exam was launched to hire for government jobs. The jobs were well paid, and open to all male citizens who could read. Parents wanted their children to read, so schools began popping up, causing a surge in literacy rates. These exams continue to this day.

Message relays

The Chinese state had a messaging system which took the Emperor's orders all across the land. The network is believed to have had more than 50,000 horses working in relays. The explorer Marco Polo wrote about it with astonishment in the 13th century, describing it as one of the 'wonders of the east

The Islamic Empire

Islam emerged as a new religion in the 7th century when the holy Qur'an was revealed to the prophet Muhammad. It spread rapidly across the Arabian Peninsula and in just 100 years the Islamic Empire had overtaken China to become the largest the world had yet seen. Its capital, Baghdad, became the largest city in the world.

The Qur'an

610 CE

The religion of Islam encourages its followers to study every letter and dot of the Qur'an for themselves. Religious imagery was considered a form of idol worship, so the text itself became the focus. Calligraphers made extraordinary letterforms and page layouts. With an emphasis on reading and learning, Islamic culture became highly literate.

Science

The followers of Islam, Muslims, believe they can find God by studying the world he created. Studying was encouraged and a huge number of scientific breakthroughs were made. Algorithms were invented, chemists identified and named many new compounds, and astronomers tracked the stars like never before. Most of the names of the stars in the night sky we use today come from Muslim astronomers.

The first public hospitals

The first public hospital, free for citizens, was founded in Baghdad in 805 CE. They soon spread across the empire. By the 10th century Baghdad had five hospitals.

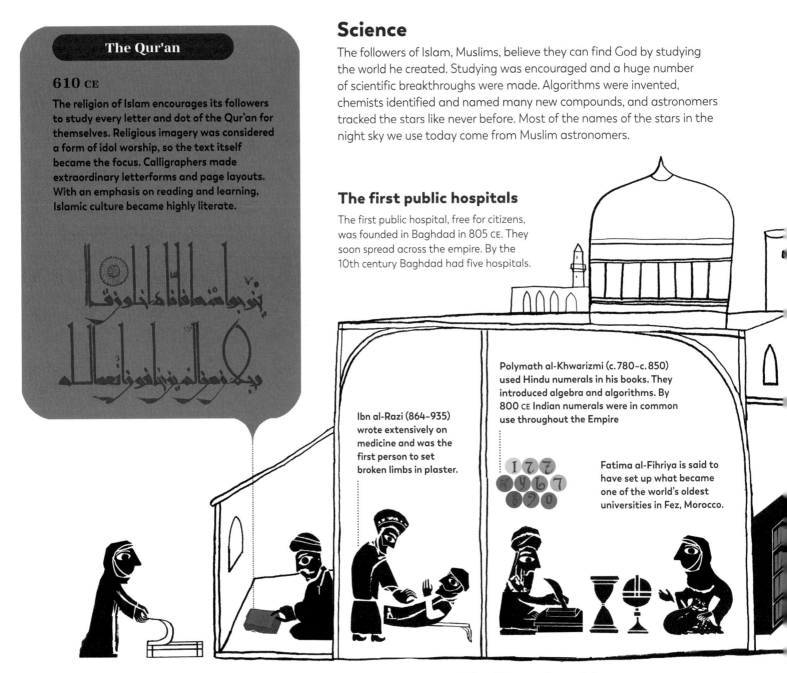

Polymath al-Khwarizmi (c. 780–c. 850) used Hindu numerals in his books. They introduced algebra and algorithms. By 800 CE Indian numerals were in common use throughout the Empire

Ibn al-Razi (864–935) wrote extensively on medicine and was the first person to set broken limbs in plaster.

Fatima al-Fihriya is said to have set up what became one of the world's oldest universities in Fez, Morocco.

The arrival of paper

Paper making was introduced to the Islamic Empire from China around 751 CE. Books could now be made more cheaply, and book traders popped up in every Muslim city.

The first universities

The Caliphs, the leaders of the Islamic Empire, set up learning institutions open to all around 850 CE. They were similar to what we now call universities. The most famous was the 'Bayt al-hikma' (House of wisdom) and 'Dar al-'ilm' (Hall of science).

Islamic geometry

While Greek thinking was mostly forgotten in Europe, the Islamic world took it and expanded it. Math and geometry were particulary admired, and seen as a path toward the divine. Islamic pattern designs are based on mathematical principles.

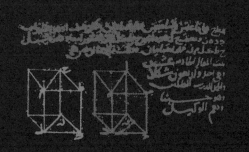

The Book of Optics

1011 CE

Ibn al-Haytham is often referred to as the Father of Science. His *Book of Optics* (p52-53) described perspective and the workings of the 'qumra' (or in Latin 'camera obscura'), proved to be hugely influential. His drawing here is the first drawing depicting a nerve.

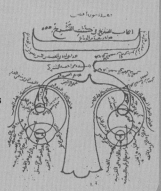

The Canon of Medicine

1025 CE

Perhaps the most influential medical book in history, Ibn Sina's book focused on the use of deduction (p57) in diagnosing illness. It was used widely in many languages throughout the world for the next 500 years.

The al-Idrisi Map

1154 CE

This was the most accurate world map of the time. Al-Idrisi also wrote books about geography and built globes.

The world's knowledge

The 'Translation Movement' was a well-funded effort to collect all knowledge. Foreigners who passed through Islamic territories were required by law to declare any books they had with them. If the book was unknown to the library it was copied and the original was returned. Books were translated from many languages, but much was from Greek and Sanskrit. The preservation of almost all surviving Greek texts today is owed to Islamic scholars.

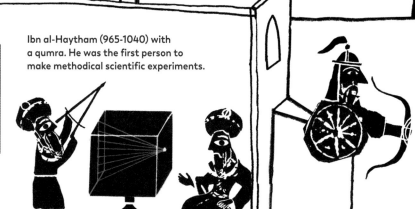

Ibn al-Haytham (965-1040) with a qumra. He was the first person to make methodical scientific experiments.

The first public libraries

By the 10th century, the world's first true public libraries appeared. Visitors were allowed to copy books. Some poor scholars earned their living by visiting the great libraries and making copies of their most important books.

The Golden Age ends

By the end of the 12th century, with internal corruption, and attacks from the Mongols in the east and Christians in the west, the Islamic Empire began to wane.

Medieval Europe

Christian Europe in the Middle Ages was largely poor and rural. The two largest cities in Europe at this time, Constantinople (present-day Istanbul) and Cordoba, were strongly influenced by Islam and cultures from outside Europe. Writing culture was dominated by the church, and literacy rates were very low.

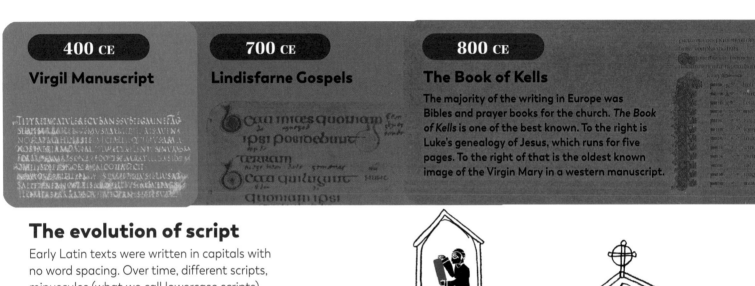

400 CE

Virgil Manuscript

700 CE

Lindisfarne Gospels

800 CE

The Book of Kells

The majority of the writing in Europe was Bibles and prayer books for the church. *The Book of Kells* is one of the best known. To the right is Luke's genealogy of Jesus, which runs for five pages. To the right of that is the oldest known image of the Virgin Mary in a western manuscript.

The evolution of script

Early Latin texts were written in capitals with no word spacing. Over time, different scripts, minuscules (what we call lowercase scripts), evolved into more fluid forms. In Britain and Ireland 'A' evolved into 'a,' while in mainland Europe it became 'a.' In the 7th century, Irish scribes who were less fluent in Latin began to add gaps between words to make it easier to read. By the 11th century, this was done all across Europe. This is highlighted in the 4th and 7th century texts above.

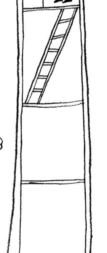

Vellum

As Christianity spread across northern Europe, papyrus, the material used to make Bibles in Rome, was not able to be grown. Instead calf skin called 'vellum' was used. A book took at least 20 calf skins to make, so books were very expensive. It is estimated a book from the time would cost more than £100,000 in today's money.

Access to books

Books were so valuable they were kept safe hidden in monasteries and churches. Most people outside the church never saw writing. In addition to the high cost, almost all the writing in Europe was in Latin. This made it twice as difficult to learn to read, because everyone had to understand Latin first.

Clerics

During this time, literacy rates were very low. Priests were the only people who could read. They were schooled by the Catholic Church. Graduates of the church schools were known as 'clerici' which is the origin of our words for both 'clergy' and office 'clerks.'

Saints

While most people were illiterate, images could still be used to communicate. The most commonly reproduced images of this time were icons of religious figures or saints. Saints were figures deemed virtuous by the church. Their often exceptional deeds were used to teach religious doctrine to the population. Sometimes these were selfless acts, but some furthered the aims of the Church, such as conversion or legitimizing the displacement or subjugation of nonbelievers. The various figures have had great influence in different ways on western culture. St. Peter brought Christianity to Rome and became the first Pope. St. Jerome translated the Bible to Latin. St. Benedict founded monasticism. St. Nicholas, known for gift giving, is known today as Santa Claus. St. George, left, known for bravery, got reimagined as a knight in medieval times and became prominent as a military saint. He is today the most common patron saint, the national saint of not only England, but also Catalonia, Ethiopia, Georgia, and Ukraine, among many other territories and organizations.

1400 CE

The Book of Hours

The *Book of Hours* became the most popular book by 1400. It contained religious texts and prayers for each hour of the day. It also listed feast days and the days of the important saints.

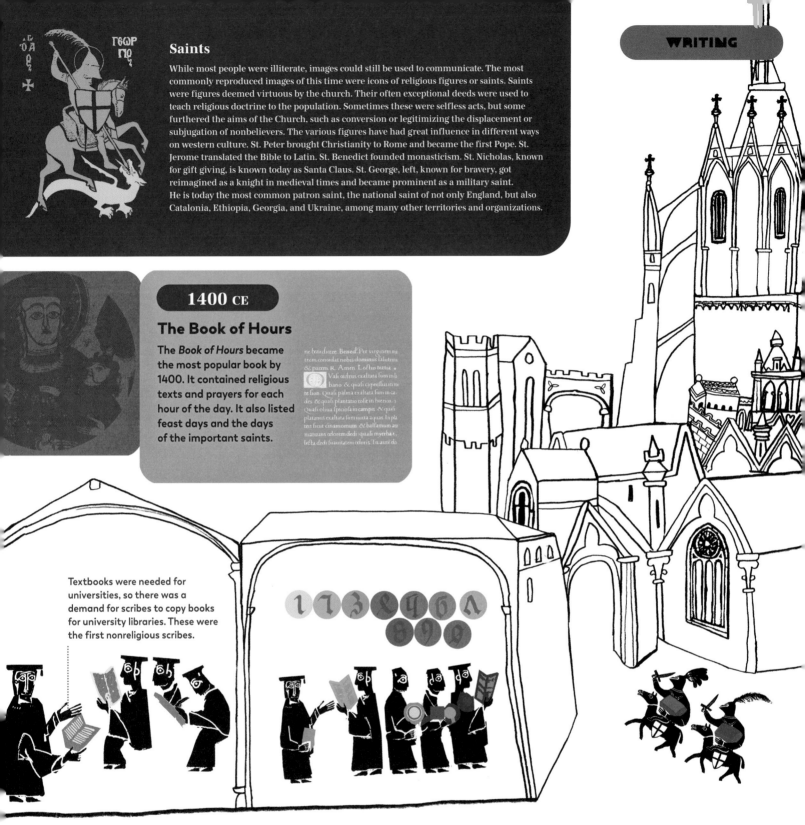

Textbooks were needed for universities, so there was a demand for scribes to copy books for university libraries. These were the first nonreligious scribes.

The first western universities

New types of independent schools emerged in the 11th century. The first was in Bologna, founded in 1088 CE. Oxford came soon after in 1096. Unlike religious schools, the students and teachers could decide what was to be studied. They were universally open to everyone, not just priests, so were called 'universities.'

Arabic numerals

Around 1100 CE, a new set of numerals (0,1,2,3...) came to Europe when Arabic mathematical texts began to be translated. They had originated in India but became known to Europeans as 'Arabic' numerals. Together with other mathematical innovations from the east, they revolutionized European mathematics.

Paper arrives in Europe

The Islamic city of Cordoba, in present-day Spain, was captured in 1236 and their paper mills began being used by Christians. Paper production soon spread. Finally, more than 1,000 years after its invention, paper had come to Christian Europe. The 'dark ages' were coming to an end. In only a few centuries, Europe would transform into the most powerful region on Earth.

The Americas

Writing, paper, and books were all invented independently in the Americas. The early Olmec civilization first developed hieroglyphic writing around 900 BCE. The Maya and Aztecs developed writing and created manuscripts written on paper. Sadly, however, almost all of this writing has been lost.

The Maya

The Maya script was the most developed writing system in the Americas. What we know about their written knowledge seems to indicate a mastery of astronomy and calendars. The Maya were truly extraordinary astronomers. One of the most important measurements in astronomy is the exact length of a year. The Maya calculation is accurate to within 13 seconds, a far closer approximation than that made any other civilization. In fact, it is even more accurate than the Gregorian calendar system we use today. It has taken western science until the 20th century to surpass the accuracy that the Maya achieved.

Math

The Maya's sophisticated mathematics included the concept of zero, which they independently invented. It was represented by a shell (below). They also developed systems that allowed them to perform complex calculations, including multiplication, division, and square roots.

The Sun King

The sun was worshipped in Mesoamerican cultures as a very powerful god. The Mesoamerican kings claimed to be descendants of gods. Some historians argue that the Mesoamerican rulers could have used their knowledge of eclipses to show power. With knowledge of future eclipses, the rulers would have been able to make it seem as though they could command the sun to dim at will.

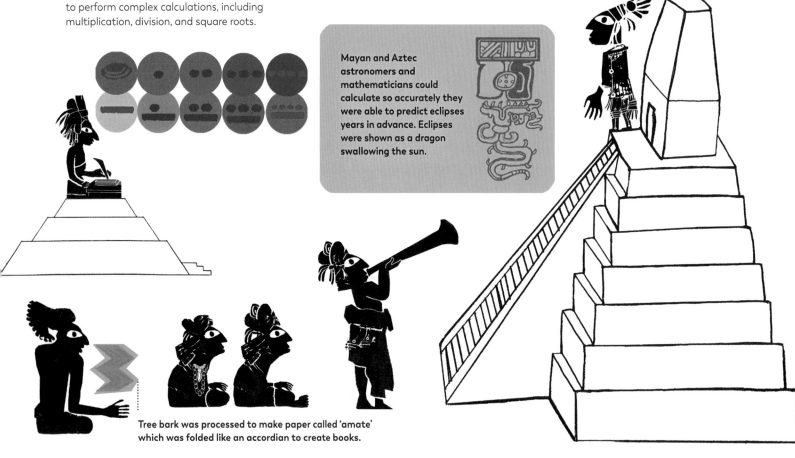

Mayan and Aztec astronomers and mathematicians could calculate so accurately they were able to predict eclipses years in advance. Eclipses were shown as a dragon swallowing the sun.

Tree bark was processed to make paper called 'amate' which was folded like an accordian to create books.

A lost legacy

The Maya and Aztecs had thousands of books on all sorts of subjects. Their histories dated back many centuries, and there were likely many other documented discoveries and histories. Sadly, they are almost all lost. The European invaders sought out and burned almost every single book. Out of thousands of Maya books, only four remain today. The number of Aztec books is only slightly more. This destruction is considered by some as the worst act of cultural desecration in history.

The four remaining Maya books are named after the places where they were kept after they were removed.

Pages from the *Dresden Codex* (note the eclipse symbol), *Madrid Codex*, *Paris Codex*, and the *Grolier Codex*.

The Aztecs

The Aztecs built great cities and were skilled astronomers. The city of Tenochtitlán (now Mexico City) was one of the largest cities in the world with an estimated 200,000–400,000 inhabitants.

The city was said to have been founded in 1325 CE to coincide with a total eclipse.

The Europeans who arrived in Tenochtitlán would never have seen a city of its size.

European conquest

In the late 1400s, tiny groups of Europeans began arriving in the Americas. These invaders had superior military technology: cannons, guns, horses, and steel swords. These, combined with the diseases they brought, meant that over the coming decades the great civilizations of the Americas would be destroyed.

Gold and silver

The Europeans made impossible demands on the local population to bring gold and silver. If such demands were not met, they or their families were brutally killed. In the first 50 years after they arrived, the Europeans took 100 tons of gold from the Americas to Europe. At the time, Europe's combined treasures amounted to around 80 tons. Europe's wealth had more than doubled in just a few decades, shifting the world's balance of power.

Christopher Columbus

Christopher Columbus was the European explorer (falsely) credited with discovering the Americas. He was a keen amateur geographer, and owned many books: Ptolemy's *Geography*, *Imago Mundi*, and *Marco Polo's Travels* among others. These books contained some of the most up to date knowledge on geography in the world. How did a lowly self-educated trader in Europe have access to the world's most up to date information? That is the subject of the next chapter.

1000 CE

Estimated world population: 300 million

The Islamic Empire is at this time the world's largest—stretching from Spain to the borders of China. The Chinese Empire to its east is also very large and technologically advanced.

Largest cities: 1. Cordoba (450,000), 2. Kaifeng, 3. Constantinople

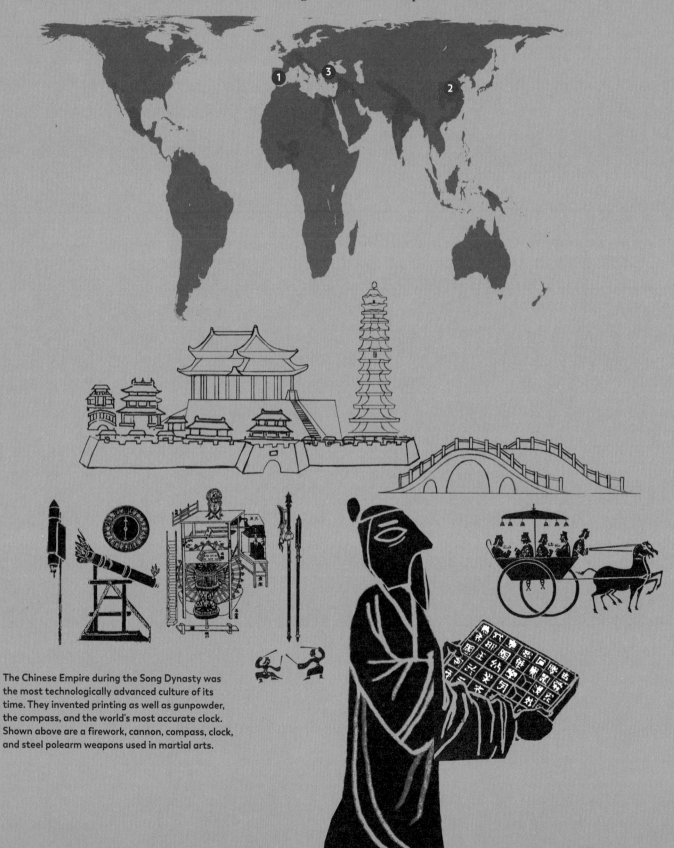

The Chinese Empire during the Song Dynasty was the most technologically advanced culture of its time. They invented printing as well as gunpowder, the compass, and the world's most accurate clock. Shown above are a firework, cannon, compass, clock, and steel polearm weapons used in martial arts.

PRINTING

"What gunpowder did for war, the printing press
has done for the mind."

–Wendell Phillips

The invention of printing

The emergence of printing revolutionized the way books were produced, making them more affordable and accessible to a wider audience. Books could be produced in large quantities, allowing knowledge and ideas to spread more quickly than ever before.

Printing

Woodblock printing was invented in ancient China around 590 CE. Images or text were carved on a wooden block, which was covered in ink and pressed onto paper. Block printing took a lot of time because the text needed to be hand carved for every page. A more efficient system, movable type printing, was later developed in Korea and China around 1040 CE. With movable type, the text didn't need to be carved each time. Reusable pre-carved characters were stored and fitted into place for each print.

First printed book

The world's first complete printed book, *The Diamond (Tantra) Sutra*, is a Buddhist text printed in China in 868 CE. The diamond in the title refers to Buddha's teachings. It is said to cut through illusions to get to 'ultimate reality.' *The Diamond That Cuts Through Illusion* is its full title.

The *Jikji*, a book of Buddhist zen teachings, was the world's first book produced by movable metal type. It was printed in Korea in 1377 CE.

First newspapers

The earliest newspaper was printed around 960 CE in Hangzhou, China. It was named *ChaoBao*, which translates as 'court paper.' It contained government announcements and official notices. Later, illegal newspapers, known as *XiaoBao*, also appeared. The government tried to ban them, but they proved too popular.

Printed materials

Ancient China had been using printed paper money, called 'flying money' from the 7th century, but from the 11th century it was widely used. It was one of the 'wonders' Marco Polo described in his travel journal. Also around this time, Chinese playing cards began arriving in Europe from the Silk Road. Europeans began printing their own cards by 1400. Gutenberg's printing press may have been inspired by these cards.

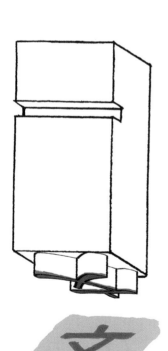

868 CE
The Diamond Sutra

960 CE
Chaobao and Xiaobao newspapers

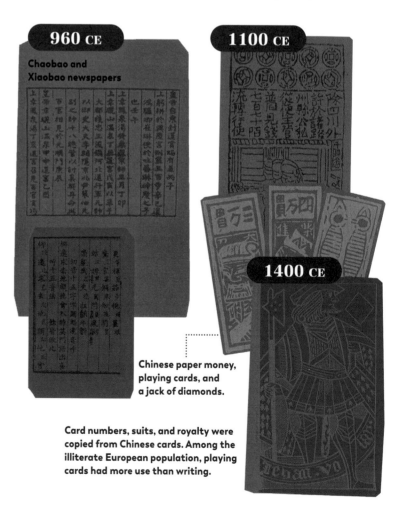

1100 CE

1400 CE

Chinese paper money, playing cards, and a jack of diamonds.

Card numbers, suits, and royalty were copied from Chinese cards. Among the illiterate European population, playing cards had more use than writing.

The rise of the west

Technological development in the West overtook the East around this time. Historians often argue about why this was. European colonization and slavery are clearly largely responsible for this, but some scholars also argue that the simplicity of the western alphabet helped printing to spread literacy, which allowed technological knowledge to be spread more easily across Europe.

Printing in East Asia

East Asian writing has so many characters that it was often easier to carve a whole new woodblock than to find the right characters. Chinese printers needed more than 8,000 different characters. Despite their early invention of movable type, most books were still printed by woodblock in China, Korea, and Japan until 1800.

Printing in Europe

In 1440 in Mainz, Germany, Johannes Gutenberg created the first movable type printing press in Europe. Compared to China's thousands of characters, Latin script has only 26 letters. This made movable type printing a far more efficient system in Europe. It spread all over the continent within 50 years, and totally transformed society. But to really see how printing was utilized in Europe, we need to understand how medieval society was organized in the late 1400s.

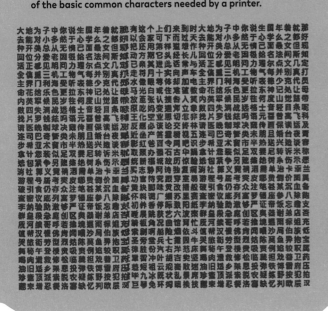

A sample of 1,000 Chinese characters. This is just 1/8th of the basic common characters needed by a printer.

The standard lettercase arrangement. Just like touch-typers today, typesetters could set type without looking, and set 1,500 letters per hour even though they were laying text in reverse.

The entire Latin script.

Elaborate wooden booths were needed to display the hundreds of character cases. Finding the right character made printing in East Asia slow and inefficient.

Latin text by contrast was arranged in only two cases: uppercase and lowercase, which is where we get these names today.

Once a page worth of text was created, a mold could be taken of it, and the characters reused. This process is known as stereotyping.

The late 1400s in Europe

Europe at this time was dominated by the Catholic Church. It was the center of all learning and literacy in Europe. The Pope was its powerful leader.

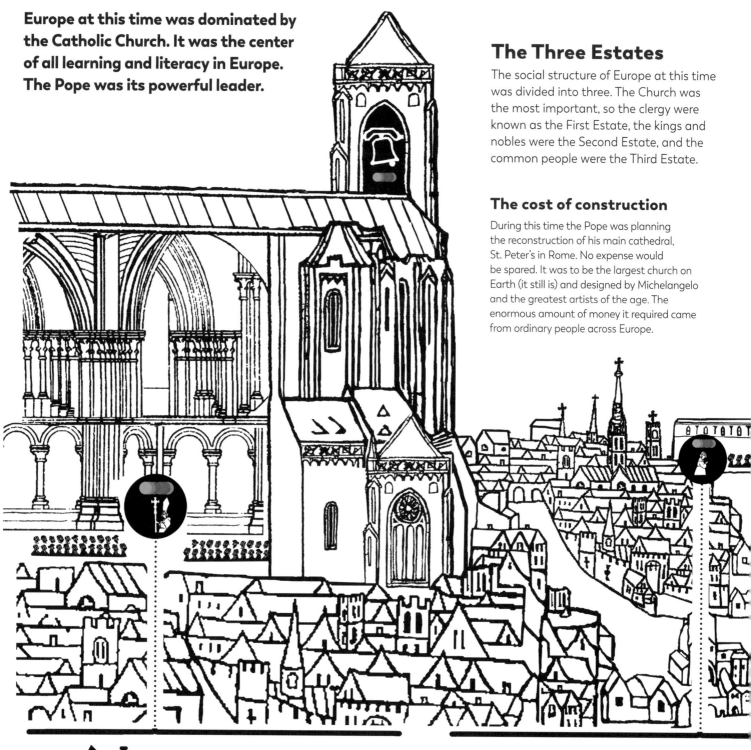

The Three Estates

The social structure of Europe at this time was divided into three. The Church was the most important, so the clergy were known as the First Estate, the kings and nobles were the Second Estate, and the common people were the Third Estate.

The cost of construction

During this time the Pope was planning the reconstruction of his main cathedral, St. Peter's in Rome. No expense would be spared. It was to be the largest church on Earth (it still is) and designed by Michelangelo and the greatest artists of the age. The enormous amount of money it required came from ordinary people across Europe.

The Pope

The Pope held authority over all of western Europe. Kings and queens across the continent competed with each other by sending gifts to the Pope in order to win favor.

Priests

There were churches in every town and village. The priest was often the most educated person in the area. They could read, write, and speak Latin. This meant they were looked up to by the villagers.

The Pope's control of Europe

The Pope held supreme religious authority over Rome and western Europe. His political authority was granted to him by the Roman Emperor Constantine in the 4th century, in a document known as *The Donation of Constantine*. However, the document was actually a forgery. This was not that unusual—there were so many forgeries at this time in Europe that it is said there were more fake documents than genuine ones. However, the scale of this fraud was remarkable. It is said to be the most important and valuable forgery in history. The fraud was exposed in 1440, further undermining the Church.

It was said that Pope Sylvester had miraculously cured Emperor Constantine of leprosy and ridded Rome of a feared dragon, so in return Constantine rewarded him with the Donation.

Funding the church

There was an extraordinary amount of corruption throughout the Church. The Church owned holy artifacts which they claimed could cure diseases and offer salvation, and charged pilgrims a fee to see or touch them. Also, the practice of 'simony,' the buying and selling of positions within the Church, was widespread.

"Listen to the voices of your dear dead relatives and friends, beseeching you and saying, 'Pity us, pity us. We are in dire torment from which you can redeem us for a pittance.'"

– Johann Tetzel, indulgence salesman

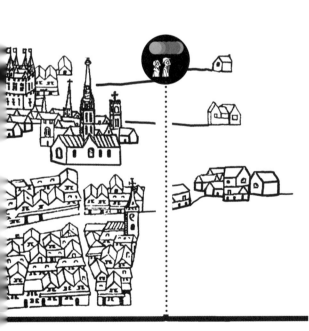

Indulgences

Much of the Church's income came from selling 'indulgences.' These were documents that the church claimed could release souls into heaven. The arrival of printing made the sale of indulgences like printing money, and made the Church very wealthy. However, some priests were growing angry with the corruption. This indulgence was printed by Gutenberg around 1454. It is one of the first examples of print in Europe.

Ordinary people

Outside of the Church almost nobody in Europe could read. There were very few books, and because rural life was very simple, there was little practical knowledge to be gained from reading.

47

The Reformation

Many people were unhappy with the corruption of the Church. In 1517, Martin Luther, a German monk and priest, set out a list of grievances in a letter to the Pope that caused a political storm across Europe.

The 95 Theses

Luther disagreed with many of the Catholic Church's practices, particularly selling indulgences. He wrote a letter that became known as 'The 95 Theses'. Luther is said to have nailed the 95 Theses to a church door. There is no actual evidence of this, but what we do know, is that he sent a copy of his letter to the Pope in Rome, and other handwritten copies to his friends. A printer friend of Luther's is known to have translated the letter from Latin to German and printed it. The Pope did not reply to Luther, but copies of the printed letter were forwarded on to other monks and priests. Many agreed with Luther's arguments, and the letter was reprinted again and again. Soon it was out of control—it had gone viral.

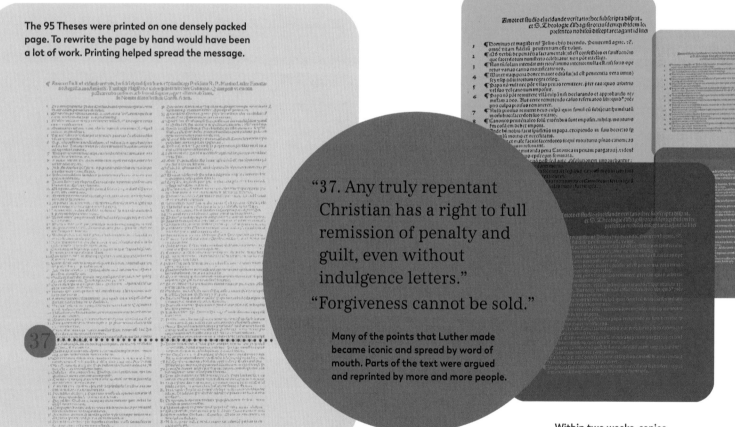

The 95 Theses were printed on one densely packed page. To rewrite the page by hand would have been a lot of work. Printing helped spread the message.

"37. Any truly repentant Christian has a right to full remission of penalty and guilt, even without indulgence letters."

"Forgiveness cannot be sold."

Many of the points that Luther made became iconic and spread by word of mouth. Parts of the text were argued and reprinted by more and more people.

Within two weeks, copies spread throughout Germany. Within two months it had spread all over Europe.

The first celebrity?

When the authorities responded to the 95 Theses, Luther responded with fire: "Your words are so foolishly and ignorantly composed that I cannot believe you understand them." He became famous for razor-sharp insults in the face of the powerful. The press could barely keep up with demand for his writings. His portrait was often printed with his words, making him one of the first internationally recognizable faces. Public debates drew enormous crowds, and students came from all across Europe to listen to his speeches.

"Your home, once the holiest of all, has become the most licentious den of thieves... the kingdom of sin, death, and hell. It is so bad that even Antichrist himself, if he should come, could think of nothing to add to its wickedness."

– Martin Luther

A bitter war of words

The Church struck back with their own letters against Luther. A furious war of words was fought with pamphlets all across Europe. But the dissenting voices had become too loud. When Luther was thrown out of the Cathloic Church he ended up founding his own church, in 1526. This is known as the Reformation, and it totally transformed Europe.

Print shops

At the time, print shops could be found in over 200 of the major European towns and cities. The use of pamphlets became the main way of spreading reformists' ideas and beliefs. Unlike the Church, they produced pamphlets in the local languages of the people, which was highly effective.

The rise of literacy in Europe

After the Reformation, a new branch of Christianity emerged: Protestanism. New churches were set up and people were encouraged to read the Bible themselves in their own language. Literacy rates grew, especially across northern Europe, and for the first time in Europe, ordinary people were learning to read.

Congregations read along with the clergy, boosting literacy. Prayer books became the most printed books, more so even than the Bible.

Medieval craftspeople were usually mobile, and sold goods in various markets. Printers had heavy equipment so needed a stationary outlet, which is where we get the word 'stationery.'

A flood of books

After the invention of printing, books became much cheaper. It is estimated they became 400 times cheaper. There were thought to be around 30,000 books in Europe before Gutenberg; which increased to around 8 million within 40 years. At first, almost all the printed books were for the Church. However, soon printers began to look elsewhere for content; classic Greek texts were revived, and books from the East were translated.

The publishing industry

Skilled manufacturers were needed to produce fine books. They needed to team up with writers, intellectuals, and foreign translators. And they needed funding from businessmen. Partnerships like this had never existed before anywhere in the world. Intellectual networks sprang up all across Europe.

New skills

Books that taught technical skills and crafts became very important. Europe saw a surge in technical knowledge, and their shipbuilding became the best in the world. Traders and craftspeople could learn the latest and best practices through books rather than having to rely on being taught firsthand. In many areas of learning there was an explosion of activity. Soon, the more literate centers of northern Europe like Amsterdam, Paris, and London, were replacing the old economic centers of Rome and Mediterranean Europe.

Joseph Moxon produced a popular series of books called *Mechanick Exercises* which introduced "The Doctrine of Handy-works applied to the Arts of Smithing, Joinery, Carpentry, Turning, Bricklayery."

Smaller and cheaper

Handwritten books tended to be large and heavy—often as much as 3ft (1 m) in size. But with printing, books could be made smaller and cheaper so more people could afford them.

bread
breade
bredde
brede

Between 1475 and about 1630, words could be spelled in all sorts of ways, and all were correct. However, with the rise of print, English spelling gradually became standardized.

The beginnings of capitalism

Most products, such as furniture, tools, and textiles were traded locally. Transportation was poor, so it made no sense to trade goods long distances when there were was local manufacturing. A book, however, is unique. If a particular title was popular, there was demand for it everywhere. Books were connecting traders in cities all over the Western world. These extending trade routes meant a financial network was needed in order to send payments. Many historians argue it was the book trade that paved the way for the rise of capitalism.

The Frankfurt Book Fair

The Frankfurt Trade Fair sold handwritten texts, among other things, from the 12th century. Gutenberg's print shop was in nearby Mainz. By 1462, the trade fair had became famous as a book fair. It rose in stature as an international fair. Today, it continues to be the world's largest book fair.

The first mass-manufactured product

Publishing became one of the first mass-manufacturing industries. Its financial success led other industries to follow suit, leading to industrialization.

The Renaissance

In 1453, the Ottoman Empire conquered and claimed the city of Constantinople (present-day Istanbul). Many European scholars left the city with ancient manuscripts. This, combined with an appetite for new books following the rise of printing, resulted in a huge boom of knowledge in Europe known as the 'Renaissance.'

An explosion of culture

Renewed interest in classical Greek and Roman culture also led to a huge shift in art, literature, science, and philosophy. Artists like Leonardo da Vinci and Michelangelo created their masterpieces, and advancements in science by Copernicus and Galileo challenged traditional beliefs and expanded our understanding of the world. Overall, the Renaissance marked a period of cultural rebirth and intellectual exploration that laid the foundation for modern Western civilization.

Ptolemy's Geography

This influential text was also brought to Europe after the fall of Constantinople. It had a big impact on the development of European mapmaking and the exploration of the Americas. Inspired by these texts, Europeans began seeking out new sea routes to Asia and beyond.

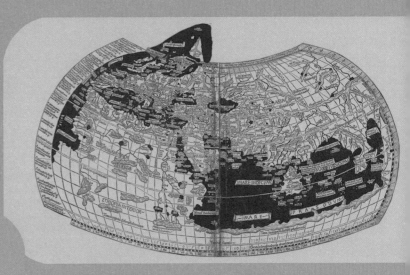

Plato and Aristotle's works

Many Greek philosophical writings were lost in Europe during the dark ages. They were brought to Europe after the fall of Constantinople. Plato and Aristotle's works in particular had a huge impact on the development of philosophy in the West, and paved the way for democracy in the centuries to come.

Leonardo Da Vinci (1452–1519)

The use of perspective in drawing by artists during this time was inspired by Ibn al-Haytham's *Book of Optics*.

The rise of literature

Ms. WILLIAM
SHAKESPEARES
COMEDIES,
HISTORIES, &
TRAGEDIES.
Published according to the
True Originall Copies.

**William Shakespeare
(1564–1616)**

Throughout this time, poetry was the preferred art form for writers. Playwriting was also a respected art form, but writing literature In Europe was considered vulgar and commercial. William Shakespeare gained his fame with a wildly popular poem, 'Venus and Adonis', which was reprinted throughout his lifetime, giving his name a boost of recognition. After his death, his plays were collected and published, which helped preserve and spread his work. By the early 1700s, the perception toward literature began to change. Government censorship of the theater and a growing literate public was helping to funnel writers toward books, and by the late 1700s fiction writing became respectable.

Imago Mundi

Another landmark book on geography, *Imago Mundi*, inspired Christopher Columbus to cross the Atlantic. Columbus himself owned a copy and he scribbled 800 notes in the margins. Columbus misunderstood the Arabic calculations that correctly showed the size of the Earth. He did not realize that the Arabic mile was much larger than the Roman mile. He was lucky. If the continent of North America did not exist between the Atlantic and Pacific Oceans, he and his crew would have almost certainly died at sea.

Euclid's Elements

Originally written in Ancient Greek in Alexandria, Egypt, this mathematical text was lost in Europe and saved by Islamic scholars. With illustrated diagrams, the printed versions became hugely influential and reawakened mathematical thought across Europe.

These notes were written by Christopher Columbus.

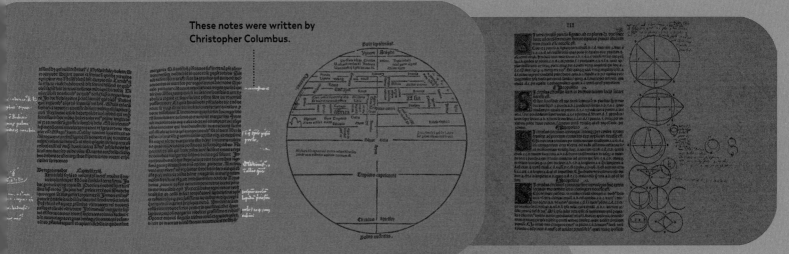

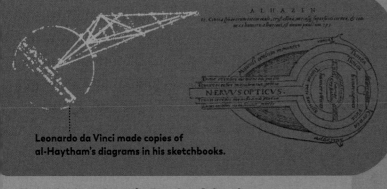

Leonardo da Vinci made copies of al-Haytham's diagrams in his sketchbooks.

Ibn al-Haytham's Book of Optics

This text had a huge influence on the west. It described the camera, perspective, and the behavior of light. It directly led to the invention of the telescope, microscope, and the use of perspective in European art.

The Great Herbal of Leonhart Fuchs

500 plant species were accurately drawn and identified in this book. These included new species from the Americas such as the pineapple, which caused a craze when it was introduced, chiles (left), as well as potatoes, corn, and tobacco. The market for new books led to a thirst for undiscovered knowledge, and a whole new discipline: science.

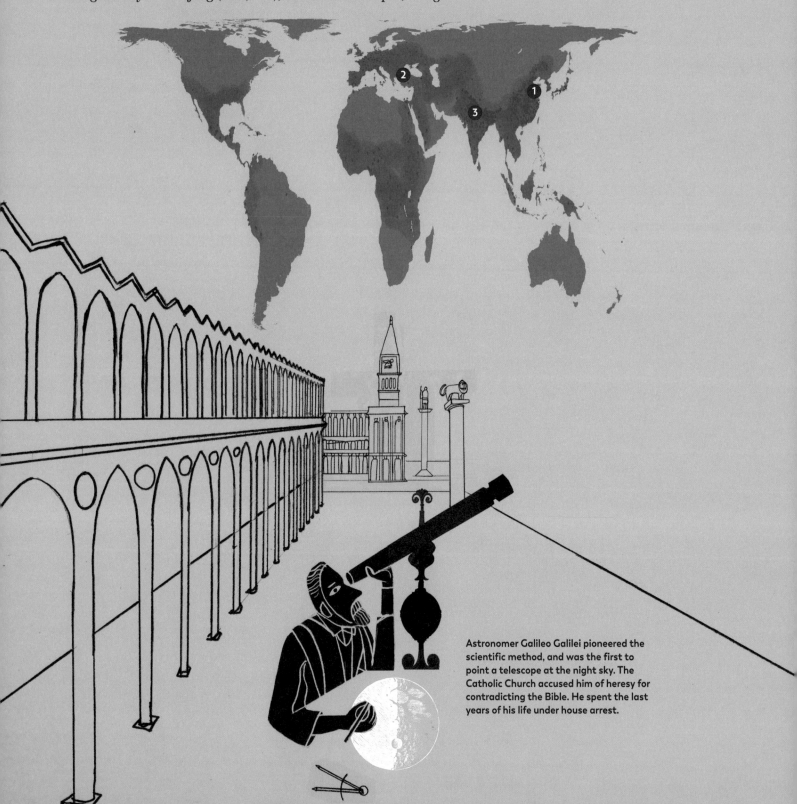

1600 CE

Estimated world population: 565 million

Venice, Italy, was one of the largest cities in Europe, but was dwarfed by the great capitals of the East. The Ming Dynasty capital, the Ottoman Empire capital, and the Mughal Empire capital were the great cities of the world.

Largest city: 1. Beijing (706,000), 2. Constantinople, 3. Agra

Astronomer Galileo Galilei pioneered the scientific method, and was the first to point a telescope at the night sky. The Catholic Church accused him of heresy for contradicting the Bible. He spent the last years of his life under house arrest.

SCIENCE

"In questions of science, the authority of a thousand is not worth the humble reasoning of a single individual."

–Galileo Galilei

The Scientific Revolution

Publishing is closely linked with the rise of science. In the 16th century, as printing took hold, specialists began seeking out books with the best and most up to date information. Publishers, in turn, sought out original content and research to publish. Soon, a new discipline began to emerge: science.

The rise of western medicine

Until the 16th century, medical knowledge in Europe was so poor that doctors usually did more harm than good. There were no medical schools, and it was usually barbers who extracted teeth and performed surgery. The Islamic world by contrast had excellent medical knowledge. A medical school was eventually founded in southern Italy. The Salerno Medical School had connections with Islamic hospitals in North Africa. They saved many lives and soon became famous. Royalty traveled there for treatment and doctors from all across Europe came to learn the schools' practices. Medical schools based on their methods soon spread across Europe.

1543

On the Fabric of the Human Body

Dissection of the human body at this time was completely unacceptable. Because of this, knowledge about the organs was very hazy. The Belgian doctor Andreas Vesalius was one of the first to dissect human bodies. His carefully observed drawings were published in a book which is considered to be the foundation of modern biology.

1614

Logarithms

Scottish mathematician John Napier published a book demonstrating a whole new way to do maths, making it far easier to do very complex calculations.

1620

Novum Organum Scientarium

British philosopher Francis Bacon proposed inductive reasoning in his landmark book. He argued that precise data should be collected, and conclusions drawn from this data alone. It became the blueprint for the scientific method.

Alchemists

Before there were scientists, there were alchemists. They believed they could create gold by mixing metals, and searched for the 'elixir of life'—a potion that could cure any illness. Many alchemists made wild claims about their abilities, and operated more like magicians or witchdoctors than scientists.

**Gottfried Leibniz
(1646-1716)**

Binary

The German scientist Gottfried Leibniz was one of the greatest mathematicians of his age. He was also one of the first Europeans to study Chinese philosophy. He was inspired by the I Ching, a text written 3,000 years ago in China. This ancient book had the insight that everything, no matter how complex, could, in theory, be composed of a combination of two opposites: yin and yang. It presented a set of 64 characters, each a unique combination of the two. Shown left are the first four of the 64 I Ching symbols. In binary, Leibniz translated them to: 000000, 100000, 010000, and 110000. He himself has scribbled the numerals they represent in green. Leibniz proposed a system of mathematics based on 0 and 1. This binary system has proved to be enormously influential. It forms the basis of all digital computing and information today. Photos, text, video, applications—no matter how complex—are all entirely made up of 0s and 1s.

1637

Discourse On Method

French philosopher René Descartes had a different method for scientific inquiry: deductive reasoning. He argued that knowledge could be attained through logic. He famously used logic to doubt everything. In the end, he arrived at the ultimate logical conclusion: "I think, therefore I am."

1666

Origine of Formes and Qualities

Robert Boyle's work, though highly flawed, set the stage for the study of matter, right down to the atomic level.

1665

Micrographia

Robert Hooke's *Micrographia* – drawings of plants and animals viewed under a microscope, became the first scientific bestseller. It coined the term 'cell'.

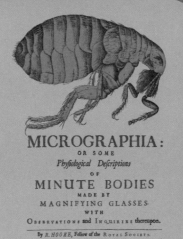

1685

Moxon's Maps

Joseph Moxon published the popular *Mechanick Exercises*. His maps and charts contained the most up to date knowledge of their time (Note the missing parts of Australia and Alaska).

1662

The Royal Society

A group of scientists in London began meeting together to share ideas. They became known as the Royal Society. They published *Philosophical Transactions*—the first ever science journal. Similar societies later sprang up throughout Europe, creating an intellectual network. Scientific research is still primarily shared through publishing. Journals allow findings to be peer reviewed and validated. Women, however, were not admitted as fellows until 1945.

The invention of the microscope (1590) and telescope (1608), in the Netherlands, had a huge impact on the understanding of the world .

Robert Hooke   Antonie van Leeuwenhoek   Edmund Halley   Isaac Newton

Data

In medieval times, each region of Europe used different units of measuring. This didn't cause much of a problem at the time since there was little trade between cities. But science depends on carefully recorded data, so there needed to be a set of standards and measuring systems in place.

Standardizing data

Weights and measures

There used to be different weighing measurements depending on what was being measured. In Rome, for example, if you were a merchant you needed one set of weights for buying gold, a different set for medicine, and another for commercial goods. Measuring length was not simple either. Lengths of cloth were measured in different units from everything else.

Time

An hour was initially a 1/12th measurement of a day and night—no matter how long the day was. This meant that daylight hours were longer in summer. This wasn't a problem since there was little need for accuracy in day to day life. However, accurate time is essential for many experiments in science.

Years

The AD/CE dating system, which counts the years since Jesus' birth, only began to be adopted in Europe in the mid 1400s. Before this, years were usually calculated from the current king's coronation year—'In the 12th year of King John'—for example. Kings and queens changed over time, and they differed from country to country, so there was almost always confusion about what year any given event happened, and most people didn't know how old they actually were!

Collecting data

In the late 1500s, London was growing quickly and needed ways to manage its population. *The Bills of Mortality* began publication in 1603. It was a single-sheet newspaper that recorded baptisms and burials in London. Clerks from each London district collected local data, and a central clerk put these together for the printers. The various causes of death were listed, which proved to be very useful. Surges in deaths gave early warning signs of disease outbreaks.

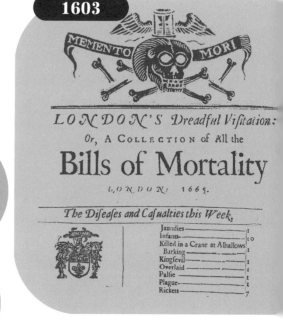

1603

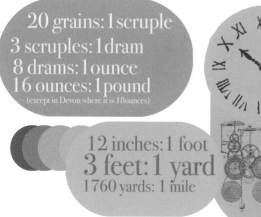

20 grains: 1 scruple
3 scruples: 1 dram
8 drams: 1 ounce
16 ounces: 1 pound
(except in Devon where it is 18 ounces)

12 inches: 1 foot
3 feet: 1 yard
1760 yards: 1 mile

The start of the year also varied. Most countries in Europe celebrated New Year's Day on January 1st, but until 1752 the UK's new year started in spring. The tax year still follows this.

1450 Anno Domini
1st January/25th March
12 hours of the day

From the 1600s, Imperial powers were colonizing the globe. Growing trade forced measurements to become standardized. These became known as 'Imperial measurements'.

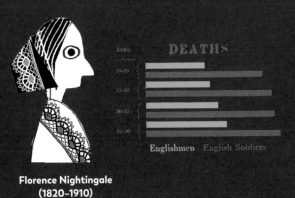

**Florence Nightingale
(1820–1910)**

Data for public awareness

Florence Nightingale used data visualizations to draw public attention to issues in medical care. Pictured here is one of her diagrams. It shows that the conditions in the British Army were so unsanitary that soldiers were dying at barracks at home in peacetime at nearly twice the rate of the civilian male population. Nightingale authored more than 200 pamphlets and reports, which led to many improvements in surgery and nursing.

Analyzing data

John Graunt, an English mathematician, analyzed the data in *The Bills of Mortality* from 1603 to 1660 and wrote a book that calculated the mortality rates of different diseases. This analysis is considered to be the first use of statistics. Graunt spotted patterns and calculated life expectancies. The statistical methods he pioneered are still the most powerful medical tools we have. Many discoveries, for example the link between lung cancer and smoking, were found by analyzing statistics alone.

Visualizing data

Raw data is difficult to make sense of. In 1669, Christiaan Huygens took Graunt's observations and made a drawing of them. It is believed to be the first visual representation of data—a graph of mortality.

The British Empire was growing rapidly. Political economist William Playfair was at the heart of its government. He created different ways to visualize the Empire's economic data. Among his innovations are the first pie charts, and line and bar charts. He is often referred to as 'the father of data visualization'.

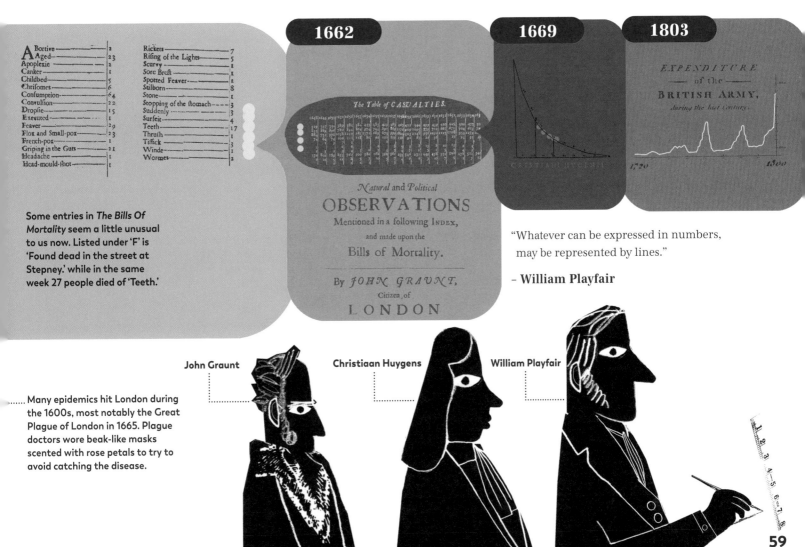

Some entries in *The Bills Of Mortality* seem a little unusual to us now. Listed under 'F' is 'Found dead in the street at Stepney.' while in the same week 27 people died of 'Teeth.'

1662

1669

1803

"Whatever can be expressed in numbers, may be represented by lines."

– **William Playfair**

Many epidemics hit London during the 1600s, most notably the Great Plague of London in 1665. Plague doctors wore beak-like masks scented with rose petals to try to avoid catching the disease.

John Graunt

Christiaan Huygens

William Playfair

Classifying knowledge

Attempts at compiling human knowledge have been made since ancient times. But it wasn't until the scientific revolution in the 18th century that encyclopedias and reference books as we know them today began to be created.

77-79 CE

Historia Naturalis

One of the first encyclopedias was created in Rome by Pliny the Elder. There are plenty of unusual entries, such as mythological creatures who 'live at the edge of the world.' It was kept alive by monks who rewrote and updated it throughout medieval times, and was one of the first classical texts to be printed.

A sciapod has "only one large foot. He uses it to shelter from the sun."

A cynocephalus has "the head of a dog, and lives at the end of the world."

1244 CE

Speculum Maius

The *Speculum Maius* (Greater Mirror) was a huge encyclopedia created by Vincent of Beauvais. With 80 volumes and 3.25 million words, it was, at the time, the largest book ever created. However its classification system was mainly based on the order of the Bible. To find a topic within its 10,000 entries, you would need to have very good Biblical knowledge. For example, animals were listed in the order they were created by God in the book of Genesis.

fish and fowl

the arts
grammar
logic
poetry
rhetoric
politics
theology

history
Creation
Adam & Eve
Egypt
Romans
Present History

natural history
God
light & the elements
sky land sea
zodiac
fish & fowl
animals
man

Pliny the Elder

Vincent of Beauvais

The Yongle Encyclopedia

The books listed here are all European. We haven't been able to include bodies of knowledge from other civilizations. Most notable is the 1408 CE *Yongle Encylopedia.* Its 11,000 volumes made it by far the world's largest general encyclopedia. It was only surpassed by Wikipedia in 2007, six centuries later. However, it was largely destroyed during the British Opium War—only 3.5 percent of it remains.

Yongle Emperor

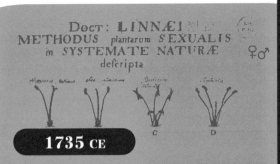

1735 CE

Systema Naturae

In this hugely influential book, Swedish biologist Carl Linnaeus categorized species—grouping animals and plants into families based on their anatomy. We still use his Latin naming structure to this day—humans are 'Homo sapiens' while domestic cats are 'Felis catus.'

Indexing

One advantage of classifying knowledge is the ease by which it can then be cross-referenced. By making connections between subjects such as geometry and physics, insights in one area can be brought to another. This effectively creates a third subject; in this case geometry and physics together created ballistics.

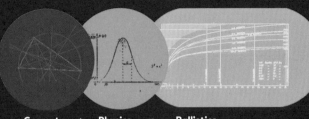

Geometry + Physics = Ballistics

1751 CE

Encyclopédie

The first modern equivalent of an encyclopedia was created by Denis Diderot in France. He hired some of the most forward-thinking intellectuals to contribute. It broke from the tradition of basing all knowledge on the Bible, and so was very controversial. Diderot printed it in secret in order to avoid the authorities, and many revolutionary ideas managed to get through due to its size. Diderot was forced to appear in court because the government challenged the entries on religion and natural order, and some of the entries were censored. Because of its revolutionary content, *Encyclopédie* is credited as being one of the inspirations behind the French Revolution.

Encyclopédie used alphabetical order, making it much easier to find topics. ....

1755 CE

Dictionary

By 1700, Latin was being used less and less. Instead, people debated the issues of the day using their national languages such as English or French. The problem was, there were no accurate agreed definitions for the words of these new languages, so there was often confusion about what was actually being discussed. All the European countries made attempts to define their languages. In England, Samuel Johnson wrote the first dictionary.

Carl Linnaeus

Denis Diderot

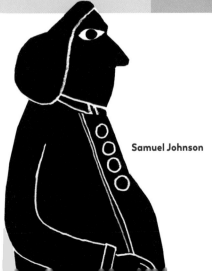

Samuel Johnson

Science: a collaboration over centuries

Science is a tool to answer questions. Many questions have been puzzled over for centuries. One of the most baffling questions in ancient times was the movement of the planets. With strange circular, looping motions, the planets behaved very differently than anything that can be seen on Earth. What were they?

Heavenly bodies

Ancient civilizations were fascinated by the planets. Many even based their gods on them. Mercury was the Greek god Hermes and Venus (p15) was Aphrodite.

Mercury
Hermes

Venus
Aphrodite

Ptolemy	Hypatia	Al-Battānī	Copernicus	Kepler	Galileo
100 CE	**400 CE**	**900 CE**	**1543 CE**	**1609 CE**	**1632 CE**
Ptolemy, a Greek astronomer, wrote *The Almagest*, a highly influential book on astronomy. It was so revered it became religious doctrine. However, it claimed the Earth was stationary and the planets and sun revolved around us.	Hypatia, a mathematician and astronomer from Alexandria, Egypt, edited and corrected *The Almagest*. She also added a better method of calculation. Others also contributed knowledge and observations.	Al-Battānī, in Syria, and others across the Islamic world, mapped the stars and the planets' paths with unprecendented accuracy. It is thanks to Islamic scholars that *The Almagest* is preserved. 'Almagest' is in fact its Arabic name.	Polish astronomer Nicolaus Copernicus used Al-Battānī's measurements for his calculations. His book *De Revolutionibus*, claimed the Earth orbits the sun. A claim so radical its title gave us the word 'revolution'.	Johannes Kepler proved that the planets do not move in circles, but in ellipses. Ellipses more closely match the planetary observations. For the first time, the planets movements could be predicted with accuracy.	Galileo Galilei used the laws of physics to perfect the orbits and show that Copernicus and Kepler were correct. He was also the first person to point a telescope at space. He saw the moons of Jupiter and the rings of Saturn, adding weight to the new theory.

"If I have seen further,
it is by standing on
the shoulders of giants".

– Isaac Newton

Science fiction

Johannes Kepler was one of the first people to realize
that the planets were, in fact, other worlds, like our
own, and that these other worlds might be inhabited.
He wrote a story about a man who travels to the moon
and sees its strange life-forms. He called it *Somnium*.
It is considered the first ever work of science fiction.

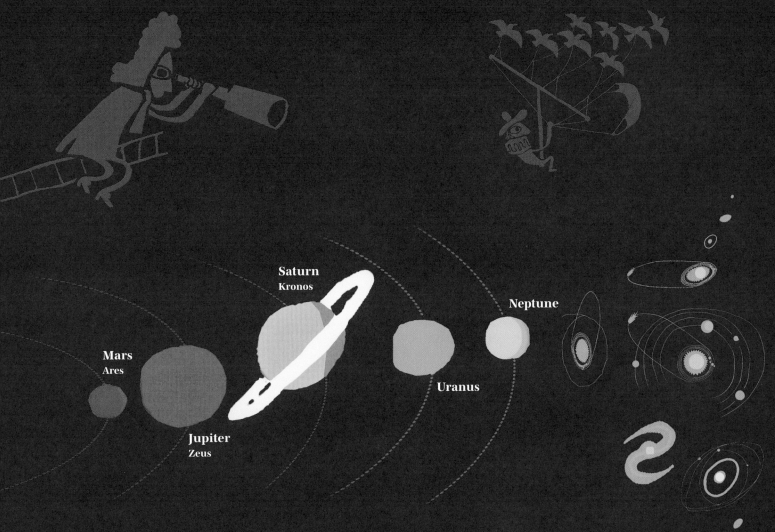

Saturn
Kronos

Neptune

Mars
Ares

Uranus

Jupiter
Zeus

Newton

1687 CE

Isaac Newton published
Principia. In it, he shows that the
movements of the planets are due
to gravity, the same forces that we
experience on Earth. The strange
movements of the planets and the
stars are no longer a mystery; they
operate under exactly the same
forces as we see on Earth.

William & Caroline Herschel

1781 CE

William Herschel, along with his sister Caroline,
discovered the distant planet Uranus with a new
telescope. As the new planet was tracked, there
was seen to be something unusual with its orbit.
Combining their observations with Newton's laws,
mathematicians concluded there must be yet
another undiscovered planet farther out, and
pinpointed where it should be found. Powerful
telescopes were eventually pointed to the position
and confirmed the planet. It was named Neptune—
the last official planet in our solar system.

The idea of progress

This was one of the first times that scientists
publicly made a prediction. It captured the
public imagination. The Herschels became
celebrities in their lifetimes. But Newton,
already long dead, became a legend. His theory
was simple but very, very powerful. Using
nothing more than some calculations with a
pencil on paper, anyone, even a school student,
could predict the movement of the planets, and
not just observable planets, but any object in
space. All the Apollo moon-landing calculations
in 1969 were made using Newton's laws.
Scientific breakthroughs like this gave rise to
a new ideology at this time that is still with us
today: the idea of 'progress.'

1700

Estimated world population: 640 million

Largest cities: 1. Constantinople (700,000), 2. Tokyo, 3. Beijing

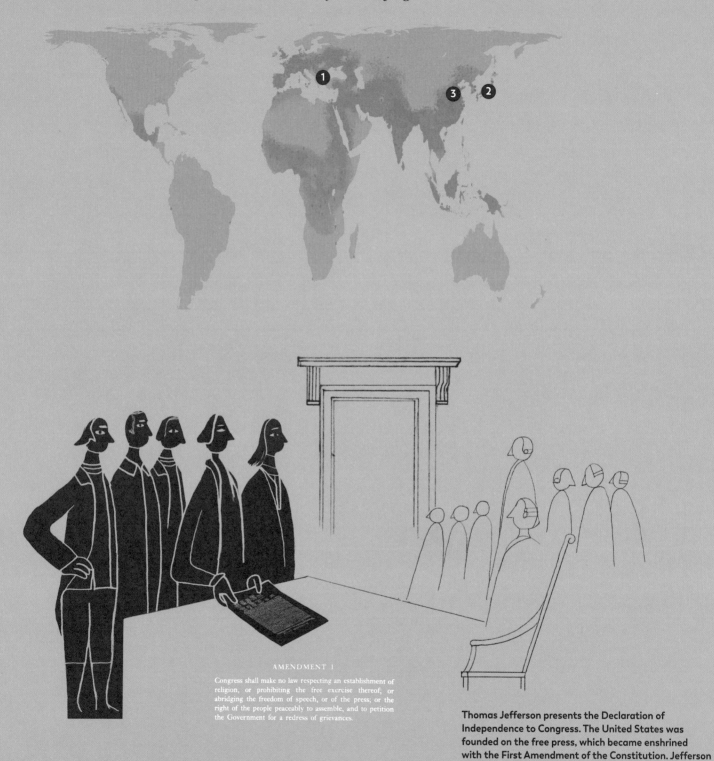

AMENDMENT 1

Congress shall make no law respecting an establishment of religion, or prohibiting the free exercise thereof; or abridging the freedom of speech, or of the press; or the right of the people peaceably to assemble, and to petition the Government for a redress of grievances.

Thomas Jefferson presents the Declaration of Independence to Congress. The United States was founded on the free press, which became enshrined with the First Amendment of the Constitution. Jefferson in his youth enthusiastically championed free speech. However during his lifetime his views changed. He and others began to fear that newspapers were becoming biased, and often spreading disinformation.

NEWS AND NEWSPAPERS

"Our liberty depends on the freedom of the press,
and that cannot be limited without being lost."

–**Thomas Jefferson**

The news

As well as books, early printers would print news stories on sheets of paper and sell them as 'news sheets.' During times of public debates, people would pay printers to print their writings. These opinions and letters were often circulated and copied from other news sheets. In this way, news spread from town to town. As their popularity grew, news sheets grew into what we now know as newspapers.

News in the past

In ancient times there was no outlet for public news. Kings or governments would send messengers if they needed to tell news of invasions or important information to nearby towns and cities. Sometimes kings would send daily relays on horseback to give orders, especially during times of war.

Gazettes

During the 16th century, the port of Venice in Italy was Europe's busiest commercial centre. Ships arriving at the port needed to spread word about their stock to the city's traders. Handwritten news sheets listing stock and prices were circulated through the city. The handwritten sheets were sold for one 'gazetta' coin, so they became known as gazettes.

Marathon

In 490 BCE, a Persian army landed in the bay of Marathon to try to conquer Greece. A messenger, Pheidippides, is said to have run the almost 26 miles from Marathon to Athens, without stopping, to deliver the news, before he collapsed and died of exhaustion. Modern marathons are based on his run as a way of remembrance.

The town square

Until newspapers emerged, people would gather in town squares to exchange or hear of news. Town criers or 'heralds' would sometimes make official announcements and would ring a bell to draw the crowd. People were sometimes publicly shamed by being put in the stocks as punishment.

Pheidippides

The earliest printed newspapers in Europe came to be known as gazettes after Venetian handwritten news sheets.

Witch hunts

Newspapers were happy to print anything that sold, and the public was fascinated by unusual or shocking reports. Gruesome reports about villains were particularly popular. All sorts of outlandish stories began to circulate. Most famous of all were stories of witches. Readers of early newspapers were mostly men, and the rush to publish more and more gruesome stories whipped the public into a paranoid frenzy. This led to trials and executions of innocent people —mostly women—labeled as witches. The trials and executions of these 'witches' in turn made fascinating news reports, and stoked fears even further. Witches and witch hunting gripped the public from around 1550 to 1700 in Europe.

The familiar images we associate with witches came from illustrations in early newspapers and pamphlets.

The first newspaper

Johann Carolus, a scribe in the city of Strasbourg, had earned a living by producing handwritten news sheets. In 1605 he acquired a printing press and began printing them instead. It was Europe's first printed newspaper, *The Relation*.

First paper in English

The first newspaper in English, the *Oxford Gazette*, was first published in Oxford, UK, but later moved to London and became known as the *London Gazette*. It was effectively a mouthpiece for the king. But it did spread word of current events.

The first daily

The first daily newspaper in English was the *Daily Courant*. It consisted of a single page with two columns and ads on the back. The focus was on reporting foreign news as reporting on home events was illegal at the time.

First papers in the US

One of the first independent newspapers in America was the *New-England Courant*. It was critical of the British government. At the time, the other newspapers in the American colonies were run by the British Government.

1605   **1665**   **1702**   **1721**

Advertisements

The first newspaper advertisements were used by printers to advertise their own books. Later, advertisements were placed by businesses, who were sometimes bullied into buying them. Newspapers would threaten business owners with running negative reports if they did not run advertisements.

The *New-England Courant* was founded by James Franklin. His brother, Benjamin, went on to become one of the Founding Fathers of the United States.

The rise of the public sphere

Ideas were spreading like wildfire across Europe. Stories of wealth from distant lands lured adventurers abroad. Exotic new foods were found in markets. Businessmen, traders, and scientists found out the latest developments through news sheets. And they got together through a new way of socializing—the coffeehouse.

Coffeehouses

Coffeehouses became very popular in England in the 1600s. At the time, it was tradition in respectable society to only meet with people they knew or had been introduced to. Coffeehouses, by contrast, were open to the public and customers were encouraged to talk to others whether they knew them or not. Coffeehouses usually had one or more long communal tables.

Penny universities

Coffeehouses were not just a place to drink coffee, but also to find out the news. They charged a penny for admission, which included access to newspapers. Most coffeehouses subscribed to three or four newspapers, and some published newspapers of their own, or had access to handwritten material too sensitive to print. So to find out what was happening, people would just pay a visit to their favorite coffeehouse.

Lloyd's of London

Lloyd's coffeehouse was a popular place for sailors, merchants, and shipowners to find the most reliable shipping news. The owner, Edward Lloyd, began publishing a sheet of shipping news: *Lloyd's List*. Traders often worried their ship would not return, so Edward began offering money to help cover the loss if the ship was lost. It led to the establishment of the first-ever insurance company, Lloyd's of London.

In the 1600s new, exotic items appeared in Europe, such as tea, coffee, tobacco, spices, potatoes, tomatoes, corn, and chocolate.

Optimism

This was a time of great optimism. One influential writer, Samuel Hartlib, wrote in 1641, "The art of printing will so spread knowledge that the common people, knowing their own rights and liberties, will not be governed by way of oppression."

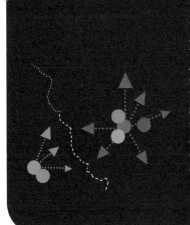

Newspapers help create nations

At this time, each city had its own distinct dialect. Languages were undefined and many national borders were not clear. Across Europe, what we would now call French dialects merged with Spanish and Catalan if traveling south. Newspapers came from the large urban centers, and when the papers of Paris spread across France, it made the Parisian dialect the language of the country: French. Likewise, London English became the language of England. In a very real sense, newspapers created countries, not only by solidifying their languages, but also by forging a national identity.

The Royal Society

Many notable scientists, including the founder of the British Museum, Hans Sloane, and Isaac Newton, debated the latest scientific findings in the Grecian Coffee House. These meetings led to the founding of the first science society, the Royal Society, and the journal the *Philosophical Transactions*.

The Bank of England

In 1694, The Bank of England was set up. This was very significant because it meant the king had to request to borrow money. His requests for money were debated and could be refused by the bank. This meant lively discussions began taking place in England; paving the way for democracy.

The Stock Exchange

The first Stock Exchange emerged in Amsterdam in 1602 with the founding of the Dutch East India Company, the first publicly traded stock company. The British East India Company followed and the London Stock Exchange emerged informally in 'Jonathan's Coffee House' in 1698.

Industrial Revolution

Networks of businessmen began to mix with networks of scientists and engineers and money began flooding into innovative ventures. The textile industry was the first to be transformed and others soon followed, leading to a time known as the Industrial Revolution.

1660 · **1694** · **1698** · **1760**

PHILOSOPHICAL TRANSACTIONS: GIVING SOME ACCOMPT OF THE PRESENT Undertakings, Studies, and Labours OF THE INGENIOUS IN MANY CONSIDERABLE PARTS OF THE WORLD

The founding document of the Bank of England

AN Interest-Book, AT 4, 5, 6, 7, 8 per C. FROM 1000 *l.* to 1 *l.* FOR 1 Day to 92 Days, and for 3, 6, 9, 12 Months. Exactly Examined, JOHN CASTAIN

Early British book and newspaper publishing was centered around Fleet Street in London.

By the early 1700s London had more coffeehouses than any other city in the western world except Constantinople.

The Age of Revolution

As well as in science and trade, radical ideas began spreading too. Before this time, most information came from authoritative sources, such as the church or monarchy. But now the public was able to circulate information among themselves. Progressive ideas about equality, liberty, and democracy were in the air. A new age was dawning: The Age of Revolution.

The Stamp Act

Monarchies across Europe worried about the free press. Their power was being challenged. The British government tried to stifle the press by introducing a tax known as the Stamp Act. They marked newspapers with a government stamp and charged a fee. It was illegal to sell a newspaper without this stamp. This deliberately hit the cheaper, more radical papers, so poor, working class readers could no longer afford them. This led to a sharp decline of the newspapers that were most critical of the Government.

The American Revolution

In 1765, the British forced the Stamp Act on the American colonies, but this time it backfired. American newspapers protested it, and spread anti-British reports, which led to the Revolutionary War. After independence, the US was a huge supporter of press freedom. Free speech and a free press is enshrined in their democracy. Rather than taxing newspapers, the government gave them subsidies. The US flooded with papers. In 1776 there were 37 newspapers in the country, but by 1830 there were more than 1,300.

The French Revolution

Imperialism was growing in Europe. While the monarchies and aristocracy had become very wealthy, the poor had only become poorer. France was the most unequal of all. Illegal pamphlets circulated. Radical ideas and news of the American Revolution eventually led to the French Revolution and the execution of King Louis XVI. After the revolution, papers became very influential. *L'Ami du Peuple* (Friend of the People) and *Le Défenseur de la Constitution* (The Defence of the Constitution) both called for the rights of the working classes.

Some papers went to great lengths to survive the Stamp Act. *Berthold's Political Handkerchief* was printed on cloth to avoid the tax.

Some papers put images of a skull and crossbones where the stamp would be placed to symbolize the death of the press.

1712

1776

1789

1787

Stamps issued by the British government to limit the free press.

The US was the first colony to win independence. The First Amendment enshrines freedom of the press.

The execution of Louis XVI and Marie Antoinette in 1793.

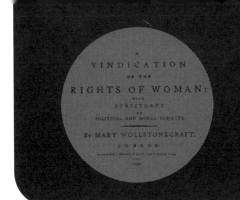

A Vindication of the Rights of Woman

In 1792, Mary Wollstonecraft published one of the earliest works on feminist philosophy. She called for women to receive an education. She argued this was not just about human rights, but about not wasting the abilities of half of humankind. "How many women thus waste life away the prey of discontentment, who might have practiced as physicians, regulated a farm, managed a shop, and stood erect, supported by their own industry."

Democracy

The revolutions sparked an intense debate all around the world. Many of the elements of modern democracy that we know today came from these discussions. Those who supported the monarchy and wanted to preserve the king's authority sat on the right in the French Assembly. Those that wanted democratic change sat on the left. This is where we get the terms left and right wing.

The Haitian Revolution

Haiti was one of the richest and most productive European colonies. It exported large amounts of bananas and sugar to the US and Europe. These were grown and harvested almost entirely by slave labor. Inspired by the events in the US and France, the enslaved people of Haiti rose up and had their own revolutionary war with France. Haiti became independent and the enslaved people were freed.

Revolutions across the western world

News of uprising sparked other major revolutions throughout the world, especially Europe and the colonies. Between 1808 and 1828 almost all of South and Central America broke free of European control. Belgium and the Netherlands had major revolutions in 1830, while Italy, Germany, the Austrian Empire, Hungary, and Poland were part of the '1848 Revolutions.'

Left and right

English political theorist Thomas Paine stood with the left. His writings *Common Sense* and *Rights of Man* were a major influence on the Founding Fathers in the US. Edmund Burke stood with the right against the revolution. These two figures are today considered the fathers of left-wing and right-wing thought.

Equality, Liberty, Fraternity?

After the Haitian Revolution, colonists worried that enslaved people in the US and elsewhere would also seek freedom. They halted all trade with Haiti. The country was thrown into turmoil. In addition, the French demanded full compensation for the freed enslaved. Haiti went from being one of the richest regions in the world to one of the poorest. Its debt to France was only paid off in 1947. Despite idealistic talk of equality, Haiti, the first truly free country, was severely punished.

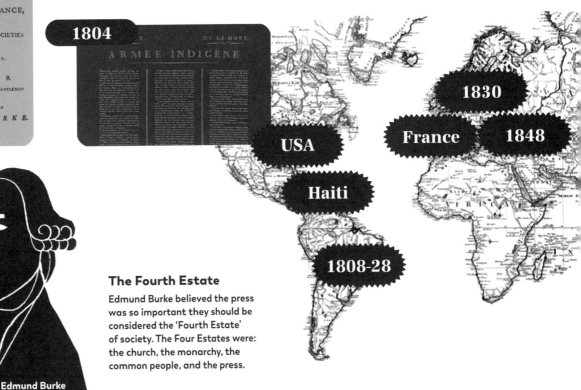

1790-91

1804

1830

France

1848

USA

Haiti

1808-28

The Fourth Estate

Edmund Burke believed the press was so important they should be considered the 'Fourth Estate' of society. The Four Estates were: the church, the monarchy, the common people, and the press.

Thomas Paine

Edmund Burke

71

Mass media

Early newspapers had small circulations. Many were specialist journals that made a profit by having the latest information on a particular industry or trade. This meant they had small specialist readerships and few advertisements. But in the US, this was all about to change.

The New York Sun

A New York printer, Benjamin Day, believed if he could print newspapers in large numbers he could sell them cheaply, and make money from ads. In 1833, he set up the *New York Sun*. Day hired a full-time writer, the first professional journalist in the US, to visit the criminal courts to pick up entertaining stories. While other newspapers sold for six or seven cents, the *Sun* sold for a penny. Advertising money soon flooded in and the paper became a roaring success. Other papers then copied this business model.

These papers became known as the 'penny press', and their type of reporting became known as 'sensationalism.'

Fact or fiction?

In 1835 *The Sun* ran a hit story that later became known as 'The Great Moon Hoax'. They claimed the astronomer John Herschel (p63) had 'built an immense telescope of an entirely new principle' and had observed a civilization on the moon. They wrote reports on the lives of the moon's inhabitants, which were descibed as 'man-bats'. It may sound unbelievable to us now, but it was believed by many people at the time.

Branding

These popular stories made *The Sun* the world's bestselling daily newspaper. Manufacturers saw the opportunities that came from such huge readerships and so started to advertise heavily. Brand names of soaps, drinks, medicines, tobacco, and other manufactured goods soon became household names. Some companies spent more on advertising than manufacturing.

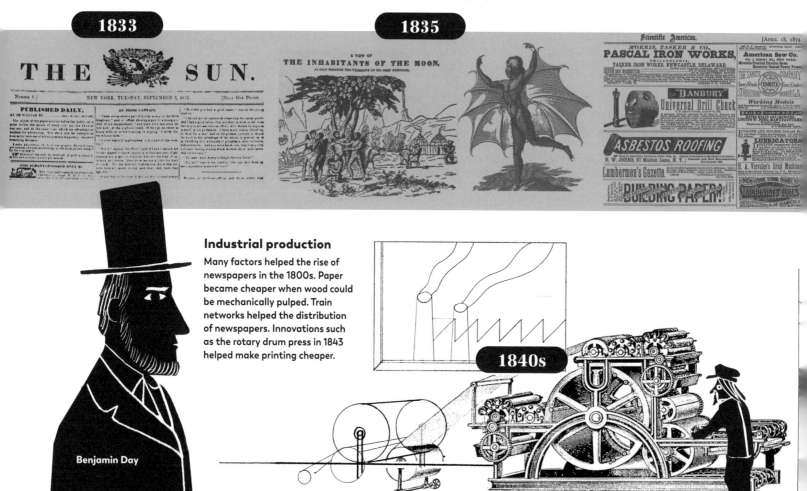

Industrial production

Many factors helped the rise of newspapers in the 1800s. Paper became cheaper when wood could be mechanically pulped. Train networks helped the distribution of newspapers. Innovations such as the rotary drum press in 1843 helped make printing cheaper.

Benjamin Day

"four score and seven years ago"

Abraham Lincoln (1809–1865)

The lettered president

It is often said it is unlikely Abraham Lincoln would become president today. He is said to have looked and behaved oddly, and spoke with a high-pitched voice in a rural accent. However, he could write extraordinarily well. His powerful speeches and letters were reprinted in the papers, and their eloquence gave him a huge following. Today he is considered one of the most popular and respected of all the American presidents.

Yellow journalism

By the end of the 19th century, two newspaper barons and rivals, Joseph Pulitzer and William Randolph Hearst, owned the two most popular papers. Pulitzer owned the *New York World* while Hearst owned the *New York Journal*. Their race for exaggerated stories became legendary. This style of journalism became known as 'yellow journalism' because they also both ran a popular called 'Yellow Kid' on the front page.

Illustration

Cartoons and caricatures were very powerful before the 20th century when there was less literacy. As one US politician said "I don't give a straw for your newspaper articles. Most of my voters can't read. But they can't help seeing those damned pictures." The US political parties were often depicted as an elephant and a donkey.

Printing images

In the early days of print, photos could not be reproduced. But Benjamin Day's son and others developed systems of dots to print photographs and images. One technique is known as 'halftone,' another is called 'Ben-Day dots.'

Spanish-American War

War also made gripping news and big sales. When rumors of political unrest began in Cuba in 1897, Hearst sent an illustrator to draw the scenes. The illustrator reported there was no conflict, and Hearst is alleged to have replied 'You furnish the pictures, I'll furnish the war.'

The USS Maine

In 1898, a ship called the *USS Maine* exploded and sank, killing 266 people. It is most likely to have been an accident with on-board gunpowder, but papers blamed the Spanish. This story and others are credited with helping lead the US into the Spanish–American War.

The New York Times

Many Americans were appalled by the actions of the press. One publisher, Adolph Ochs, was so horrified by the sensationalist reporting that he bought the *New York Times* in 1896 with a vision to provide a more reliable news alternative.

Halftone dots   **Ben-Day dots**

The Spanish-American War led to unprecedented sales for both papers.

1880-90s

1898

1896

1880

The 'Yellow Kid' is often credited as the world's first comic strip, and is among the very first images printed in color. The character was based on a cheeky Irish immigrant child from the New York ghettos.

Joseph Pulitzer

William Randolph Hearst

Newsboys

Hiring 'newsboys' was another tactic by Benjamin Day that Hearst and Pulitzer copied. The boys made small earnings by buying bundles of papers for half a cent each and selling them for a penny.

The modern press

The US may have pioneered the mass media but the British copied the model and surpassed it. By the end of the 19th century, and for much of the 20th century, the largest newspaper circulations in the world were British. And they invented a new newspaper format: the tabloid.

Broadsheets

The *Times of London* was the world's largest-selling newspaper for much of the 19th century. Independent and often critical of the government, it was respected around the world. The *Manchester Guardian*, founded in 1821, and other papers began competing for readers in the later half of the century.

The Crimean War

One of the best known *Times* reporters, William Howard Russell, published damning accounts of the Crimean War in the 1850s. The public was outraged and his reporting contributed to the collapse of the government, as well as inspiring Florence Nightingale and others to go to Crimea to help the wounded on the battlefield.

1785

1821

1842

1855

1860s

Price and speed

Huge, expensive printing presses were needed to compete in the newspaper business.

The press barons

The early 20th century was dominated by 'press barons' who owned the major newspapers. These wealthy businessmen had business links across the British Empire, and used their papers to extend their power and business interests.

Daily Mail & Daily Mirror

In 1896, the *London Daily Mail* was launched by brothers Lord Northcliffe and Viscount Rothermere. It was aimed at the newly literate lower-middle class. It was cheaper than competitors, which was made possible by advertising. During the Boer War of 1899–1902 it sold more than a million copies a day. Lord Northcliffe later introduced the world's first tabloid, the *Daily Mirror* in 1903.

The Daily Express

Lord Beaverbrook later became the most prominent of the barons. His *Express* newspaper became the largest-circulation newspaper in the world in the early 20th century. During WWI he was made the first 'Minister of Information' in charge of British propaganda messaging.

By the 1920s, the barons got into politics themselves. Rothermere and Beaverbrook eventually joined forces to create the 'United Empire Party' to further their business interests and that of the British Empire.

1896

1903

1900

Viscount Rothermere   **Lord Northcliffe**   **Lord Beaverbrook**

After the wars, newspapers engaged in a race to gain the most readers. Serious news was often dropped in favor of popular gossip stories and sports.

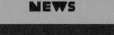

The free press

Democracy relies on a free press. As theorists on both the left and right have argued, voters must have full information about the actions of their governments. Consumers too, have the right to know what the businesses they support are doing behind closed doors. The public should know what is being done in their name—both good and bad—if there are to be honest debates and an informed vote. We rely on the media to uncover uncomfortable truths and keep a check on those in power. However, we have allowed our media to be almost exclusively owned by billionaires. Media ownership is usually not lucrative, and many newspapers even run at a loss. The reason these wealthy businessmen want to own media outlets is to protect their business interests and shape public opinion in their favor. Is it right that we have allowed the media to be owned in this way?

Deregulation

Beginning in the 1980s, the UK, US, and other countries began loosening regulation on the media. Laws that had been in place to ensure—among other things—equal airtime for public office seekers, were abolished in 1987. In 1996, the Telecommunications Act was introduced, allowing corporations to buy up media markets. Before the Act, approximately 50 companies controlled 90 percent of the media and entertainment industries; today only five or six corporations control the same market share. Similar laws have been introduced around the world.

Newpapers today

Today it is newspapers in Asia that have the largest circulations. The *Yomiuri Shimbun* in Japan, and *Times of India*, are some of the most-read. In recent years, there have been huge changes in news media. Media ownership is consolidating even further. Some of the most widely read newspapers today are entirely free of charge. They are often given out at subway stations in large cities, and are funded by advertising alone. But by far the biggest change is the rise of online news.

Tabloids

Tabloid papers are smaller in size, and tend to focus on celebrity news, gossip, and scandals. As well as selling papers, scandals can shape public opinion, especially in politics.

Online news

Since the mid 1990s, the Internet began replacing newspapers as people's main information source, causing print sales to fall dramatically. This has accelerated in recent years with the rise of social media. These new media forms are transforming the way news is produced and consumed, and creating new business models for journalism.

1969

1999

Rupert Murdoch

Businessman Rupert Murdoch was perhaps the greatest beneficiary of deregulation laws. He bought hundreds of newspapers around the world, as well as TV broadcasting channels and other media interests.

Rupert Murdoch

Photography

In the 19th century, Paris was the cultural capital of the world. It hosted exhibitions showcasing marvels like the Eiffel Tower, and artists came from all over to live and work in the city. But the art world was in for a shock. Photography, perhaps the most important invention since printing, was about to change visual culture forever.

Early photography

During the early days of photography, different processes competed against each other. The Daguerreotype, a one-off image on a metal plate invented in France by Louis Daguerre, proved to be the most popular early on. Later, the English scientist William Henry Fox Talbot invented the first paper-printing photograph, which eventually took over.

Photojournalism

The public became gripped by photographs of the things they had never seen before: famous people they had read about, distant lands, and events. Photographers began traveling to capture images, and photojournalism was born.

Photos of the recently deceased were common. People were rarely photographed, so it was often the only way to remember them.

1826

This is the world's first photographic image. It was captured by inventor Nicéphore Niépce over several days of exposure from his studio in France.

1840s

This Daguerreotype is of Louis Daguerre himself. Exposure times reduced from around 20 minutes in the 1840s to 20 seconds by the 1860s.

The Crimean War

Roger Fenton and Carol Szathmari are considered the first war photojournalists for their work in Crimea. Photos could not yet be printed in newspapers so their images were shown in touring exhibitions. There were no action shots, and the images were posed, but despite this, images of battlefields brought an awareness of war to the public for the first time.

Fenton needed a huge horse-drawn wagon as a lab. It took him 3 months to take 360 photos.

Roger Fenton
1819–1869

1850s

Modern art

Before the invention of photography, it was the job of artists to visually record events and capture likenesses. The low cost of photography compared to formal painted portraits meant artists could no longer compete in the same way. From the 1860s onward, some artists began experimenting with new ways of expression, and modern art was born.

Printing photos

The invention of the halftone process in the 1880s allowed photographic images to be printed for the first time. Suddenly, photos became part of everyday life, and they began to appear in newspapers, magazines, and posters.

1936

THE NEW YORKER

1925

TIME

1923

Life

Life magazine relaunched in 1936 with a focus on photography. This image from D-Day is by one of the best-known war photographers, Robert Capa, who was later killed in Vietnam. *Marie-Claire*, *Elle*, and later, in 1965, *Cosmopolitan* became some of the world's bestselling titles.

In 1913, *Vogue* magazine began publishing photos by the first fashion photographer, Baron Adolph de Meyer.

National Geographic

National Geographic quickly distinguished itself with high-quality, photographic essays of distant places.

VOGUE

MARIE-CLAIRE ELLE

1888

1892

1937

1945

LUMIÈRES

CINEMATOGRAPHE

Charlie CHAPLIN
...in One of the Funniest Comedies of All Time!
"CITY LIGHTS"

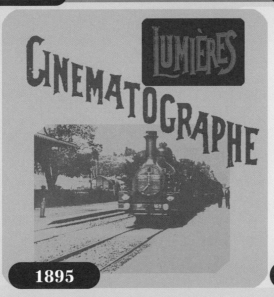

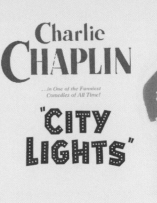

1870s

1895

1890s-1920s

Eadweard Muybridge conducted motion studies in the late 1870s using multiple cameras for the first time.

The beginnings of cinema

Different ways of showing films were trialed. American inventor Thomas Edison (p87) created 'kinetoscopes,' private booths where one viewer could watch short films. In France, the Lumière brothers showed films in dark rooms called 'cinematographes.' Audiences gasped in awe at films as simple as a train arriving at a station. The cinematographe won out.

Silent film

Silent films were produced from the late 1890s to the late 1920s. Early cameras needed bright sunlight to operate, so they chose to locate film studios in California. The film industry was beginning, and its center was not Paris, London, or New York—it was Hollywood.

Intellectual property

A few centuries ago, a new idea emerged: the idea of owning information. There are currently three different ways to own information: through patents, copyrights, and trademarks. These 'intellectual properties' have grown so much in importance that today they account for around 40 percent of the US economy. How did this idea of ownership come about?

Censorship

In most countries, copyright began as censorship. From the 1640s, England was undergoing huge political change, and publishing was seen as a threat to the government. In 1662, the government passed a law where publishers needed to apply for a license to print a book. If the government granted this license, that publisher would hold a 'copyright' on it, making it illegal for any other publisher to publish that particular book.

Copyright for books

Over time, censorship laws began to relax. But publishers did not want to give up their valuable copyright, and wanted to keep the law in place, arguing the benefits of copyright for the author. The 'Statute of Anne' was passed in 1710, which allowed publishers to keep their copyright. It also extended copyright to the authors so that they had ownership of their work.

The law worked well for the government, but also for the publishers. If they had copyright to a popular book it became very lucrative.

Copyright for images

William Hogarth was one of the best-known visual artists of his time. His work was sold as prints. However, many printers made unauthorized copies of his work. Hogarth and other artists pressured the government to pass the 'Engraving Act' in 1735, which gave them copyright for 14 years.

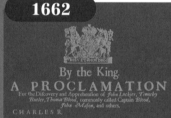

1662

By the King.
A PROCLAMATION
For the Discovery and Apprehension of *John Lockier, Tymothy Butler, Thomas Blood,* commonly called Captain Blood, *John Mason,* and others.

CHARLES R.

1710

Anno Octavo
Annæ Reginæ.

An Act for the Encouragement of Learning, by Vesting the Copies of Printed Books in the Authors or Purchasers of such Copies, during the Times therein mentioned.

1735

Anno octavo GEORGII II.

After 24 June, 1735, the property of historical and other prints vested in the inventor for 14 years.

Patents

If an invention is innovative, it may be eligible for patent protection. This allows the inventor to have exclusive rights on their invention for a limited time, while allowing the invention to be made public. The Venetian Republic established the earliest known patent systems.

The first patent

The first recorded patent is believed to be from 1421, when Florence granted one to engineer Filippo Brunelleschi for a method of transporting pieces of marble. He was awarded three years to have sole use of his technique. Later, during the Industrial Revolution, industrialists pushed for stronger patent systems.

Brunelleschi designed the Florence Cathedral Dome. The inspiration for many revered buildings: St Peters, St Pauls, and the US Capitol.

Filippo Brunelleschi 1377–1446

William Hogarth 1697–1764

Trademarks

Marks to identify manufacturers have been around since ancient times. But in the 19th century, businesses began recognizing the importance of branding, and fought to protect infringements. Today, much of the value of a company is in its trademark. Coca-Cola, for instance, does not hold a patent on its recipe. Other manufacturers can make similar cola drinks, but cannot infringe on the trademark.

Pictured below is the first registered trademark—the red triangle trademark of Bass and Co. Pale Ale.

TM

®

1876

Is copyright really a good thing?

Intellectual property protections are said to encourage innovation, but much of its history suggests the opposite. Today, the terms of copyright last for 70 years after a creator's death. This benefits large media companies, not cash-strapped innovators. Can copyright laws be redesigned so that they reward the work of innovators and benefit society as a whole? Some groups, such as the copyleft movement, aim to make copyright fairer.

Copyright in the US

There was not much copyright protection in the US in the early 1800s because there were very few successful American creators at the time and American society benefited from cheaper royalty-free European books and ideas.

Charles Dickens

Charles Dickens was perhaps the most famous author of his time. His books sold millions in the US, but he earned nothing from them. He was outspoken about copyright his whole life, but the law was not changed in his lifetime.

US Copyright laws

Toward the end of the 19th century, the US went from being an importer of copyrighted works to being an exporter, and the US became the leading enforcer of copyright law worldwide. Today, nearly half of the US economy comes from intellectual copyright protections. China has since followed suit, with a near identical path from being a copyright-free territory in the 1980s to enforcing copyright protection today.

Copyright terms

Walt Disney created 'Steamboat Willie,' the world's first animated film with synchronized sound, in 1928. It featured the talking character Mickey Mouse. Mickey became a global sensation, and Disney produced many more films with him. The Walt Disney company became concerned that the 14-year copyright on their character would soon run out, so they put pressure on the US government to extend the term. The copyright term, nicknamed the 'Mickey Mouse Protection Act,' now lasts 70 years after the creator's death.

Copyright today

Today, notions of copyright are again being challenged. Our personal data is being collected by social media companies, while AI harvests enormous amounts of content without permission.

Richard Stallman

Computer scientist Richard Stallman developed the concept of copyleft (see box above) and the free software movement. The GNU/Linux operating system was also pioneered by Stallman in 1984. It is the most widely used operating system in the world.

1845

"Only in this way can we protect intellectual property, the labors of the mind, productions and interests are as much a man's own... as the wheat he cultivates, or the flocks he rears."

—**Massachusetts Court Ruling**

1928

Mickey Mouse's copyright finally expired in 2024. Walt Disney was a pioneer of his time. He won more Oscars than any other individual.

1984

1909

The copyright mark was introduced in 1909 as a shorthand for the 'copyright notice'. Books still use the copyright notice. It can be seen in the first pages of this book.

Charles Dickens
1812–1870

Walt Disney
1901–1966

Richard Stallman
1953–

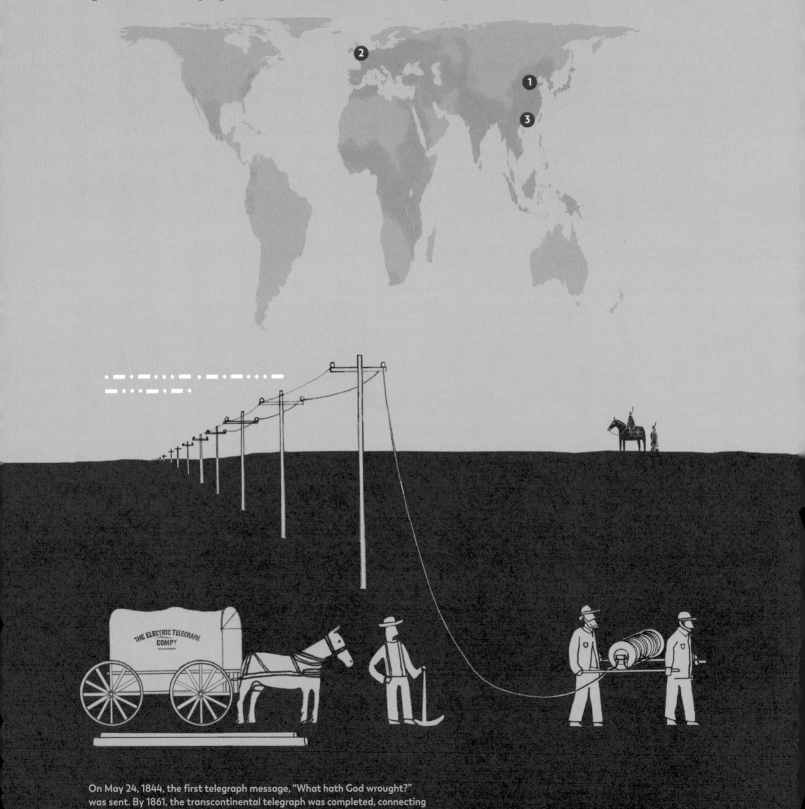

1800

Estimated world population: 970 million
Largest cities: 1. Beijing (1.1 million), 2. London, 3. Guangzhou

On May 24, 1844, the first telegraph message, "What hath God wrought?"
was sent. By 1861, the transcontinental telegraph was completed, connecting
the East and West coasts, and transforming communications across the
country. Telegraph lines form the basis of today's Internet.

NETWORKS

"[It would not be long] ere the whole surface of this country would be channeled for those nerves which are to diffuse, with the speed of thought, a knowledge of all that is occurring throughout the land, making, in fact, one neighborhood of the whole country."

—Samuel Morse

Mail

Messaging networks have existed since ancient times. But it was only royalty that were able to send mail with these early systems. Royal orders were sent across the kingdom, or diplomatic messages to foreign lands. However, as new networks developed, they began to open up to the public and create the postal system.

Ancient messaging

Early messages were carried on foot or by horseback. It was slow, grueling work. Around 500 BCE, the Persian Empire (Iran) created the most sophisticated relay system of its time. Mail stations were spaced a day's ride apart (about 155 miles) across a network running from Greece to India. The main route, called the 'Royal road' took 90 days to walk, but a message took only nine days.

All roads lead to Rome

Rome copied the Persian system and named it the 'cursus publicus.' It was essential to the running of the Roman Empire. They built 50,000 miles of high-quality roads to help with fast messaging. Until modern times, the road network and the communication network were one and the same.

Merchant networks

Merchant networks began springing up across Europe in the late Middle Ages. In contrast to royal messenger systems, these networks would carry messages for a fee. Trade routes, such as the Silk Road between Europe and Asia, brought messages in addition to silk and other goods.

The mail coach

Around 1650, mail coaches started allowing passengers onboard. It was the fastest way to travel until railroads were built in the mid 19th century. However, their regular times and routes made them targets for robberies by highwaymen, and the wealthy passengers were held at ransom.

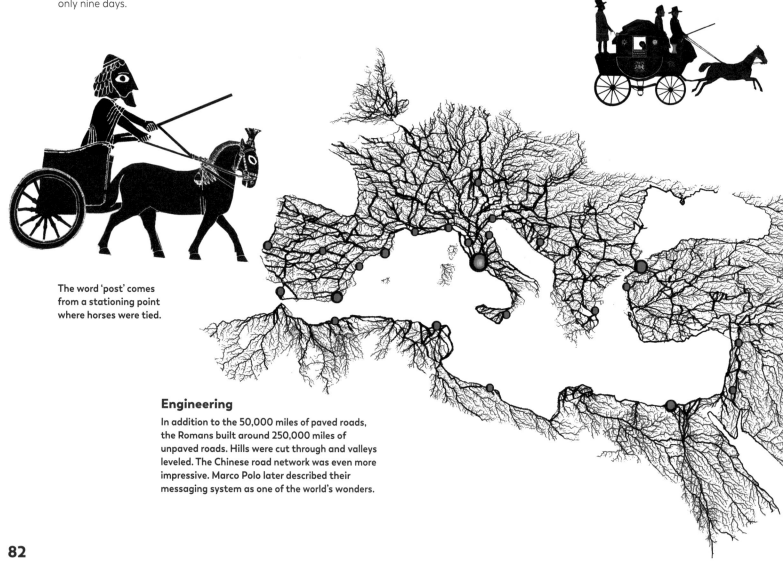

The word 'post' comes from a stationing point where horses were tied.

Engineering

In addition to the 50,000 miles of paved roads, the Romans built around 250,000 miles of unpaved roads. Hills were cut through and valleys leveled. The Chinese road network was even more impressive. Marco Polo later described their messaging system as one of the world's wonders.

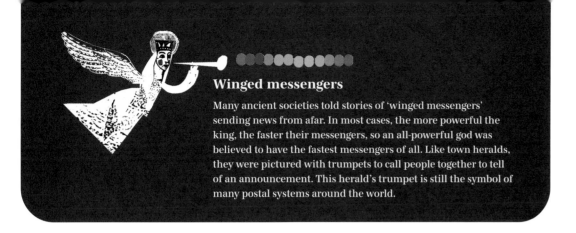

Winged messengers

Many ancient societies told stories of 'winged messengers' sending news from afar. In most cases, the more powerful the king, the faster their messengers, so an all-powerful god was believed to have the fastest messengers of all. Like town heralds, they were pictured with trumpets to call people together to tell of an announcement. This herald's trumpet is still the symbol of many postal systems around the world.

Modern postal system

The railroad networks sped up postal delivery enormously, but the postal system was complicated and expensive. Prices depended on many factors, such as weight, destination, and chosen route. This was a particular problem for the huge British Empire, where mail was being sent all over the world. A radical postal reform in 1840 made the process simpler and cheaper.

The first stamps

As part of this reform, the postage 'stamp' was introduced. One letter was charged at one penny (around $1.25 today). This made mail cheap and easy to send. Letter-writing became popular, and the volume of mail increased dramatically. In the following 20 years, 90 other countries followed the flat-rate prepaid postage system. Collectively, they created the modern postal system.

Mass mail

The tradition of sending Christmas cards began soon after stamps were introduced. The public was encouraged to make use of the postal system. Valentine's Day as we know it today was largely an invention of the postal system to encourage the sending of cards. Advertisers also began sending unsolicited mail.

Alfred Russel Wallace
(1823–1913)

Charles Darwin

Charles Darwin was a prolific letter-writer. He wrote to more than 2,000 people around the world, including geologists, biologists, and even pigeon breeders. He had a theory about how life evolved, but spent years delaying publication.

Alfred Russel Wallace

In 1858, Darwin received a letter from Indonesia sent by naturalist Alfred Russel Wallace. In the letter, Wallace described to Darwin his theory of evolution. To Darwin's horror, it was the same as his own. Darwin immediately published the theory and co-credited Wallace. Their theory is considered by many to be the greatest scientific discovery of all time.

The Royal Mail

At its peak, Britain's Royal Mail was processing 4 million letters a day in London alone and Londoners would complain if their letter was not delivered within hours. By the beginning of WWI, the Royal Mail was the largest employer in Britain. However, by this time the mail was being replaced with a radical new technology: the telegraph.

Charles Darwin
(1809–1882)

The telegraph

The introduction of the telegraph caused a big shock to society. Before this time, the fastest messages were only as fast as a horse or train—not much different than in ancient times. But with the telegraph, information could be sent instantly. The fastest transatlantic messages, which had taken more than five days, now took 0.3 seconds.

Optical telegraph

The precursor to the telegraph was the optical telegraph or 'flag semaphore.' Pioneered by French engineer Claude Chappe, the system operated by transmitting messages between towers by sight. Operators used telescopes, and relayed the signals with flags. A network of hundreds of miles was installed across France during Napoleon's time. However it had many limitations, so an alternative using electricity was proposed.

Morse

The first electrical telegraph systems in the 1830s used several cables that each operated a pointer to spell out words. Samuel Morse proposed a much simpler system with just one cable, and publicly demonstrated it in 1844. Using a sequence of dots and dashes he could spell out numbers and letters. His simple system ultimately became the international standard.

Press agencies

Telegraph operators sent and received news. Soon, press agencies, or wire services, were set up. Havas/Agence France-Presse (1835), Associated Press (1846), and Reuters Telegram Company (1851) gathered news stories and sent them by telegram to newspapers. Objectivity was a large selling point for these businesses, as they sold to different countries with different politics. Facts such as quotes and sports scores could be used by all. The public was enthralled with this instant worldwide news. Many newspapers began using 'telegraph' in their names.

**Samuel Morse
(1791–1872)**

S.O.S

Three dots, three dashes, three dots was made the international distress signal in 1906. Its simple repetitive signal meant it could be understood by anyone.

New York London Moscow Beijing Tokyo Sydney

Standardizing time

Before the railroads arrived, each town worked to their own local time. This was a problem for rail travel since the rail system needed accurate clocks for safety. But the expanding telegraph networks provided the solution. From the 1850s, clocks were set by time signals sent from Greenwich in London to all of Britain. International time standards faced a similar problem; as communication became instant around the world, a world time was called for. An international conference in 1884, held in Washington DC, agreed on setting the world time zones.

Connecting the empire

Britain, as the center of the world's largest empire, invested heavily in laying cables. It subsidized companies to connect the empire by telegraph. A cable laid beneath the English Channel in 1850 successfully relayed several messages, but it failed within hours. In 1858, a huge underwater cable thousands of miles long was laid to connect Europe with America. It also failed within weeks, but the cables were relaid and soon the entire world was connected by telegraph.

The stock market

Once messages could be sent at distance, money soon followed. Western Union began as a telegraph company, but shifted into long-distance money transfers. Cable telegraphy became a huge boon for business as investments in distant markets could be made by telegram. In the 1860s, the first stock tickers appeared; which were telegraphic printing machines transmitting real-time stock price information over telegraph lines. The stock ticker on TV financial news today is derived from these tickers.

World trade was stimulated and the stock market boomed for a time. However, prices fell suddenly on the New York Stock Exchange in October 1929—the telegraph lines carrying financial information could not keep up with the frantic selling.

Electrifying the voice

Sending messages by telegraph was not easy. Messages needed to be encoded and decoded. Engineers believed there would soon be a way to electrify the voice. So, in the 1860s and 70s engineers and inventors began a race. Everyone was trying to solve the puzzle: How can sound be converted into electricity?

The end of war?

People had once imagined that instant communication would end war forever. However, that didn't happen. In fact, the Prussian statesman Otto Von Bismarck was said to have started the Franco-Prussian War with a telegram in 1870.

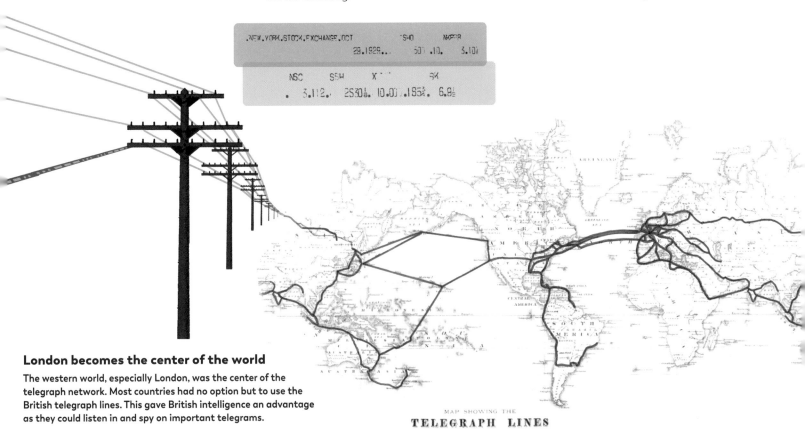

MAP SHOWING THE
TELEGRAPH LINES

London becomes the center of the world

The western world, especially London, was the center of the telegraph network. Most countries had no option but to use the British telegraph lines. This gave British intelligence an advantage as they could listen in and spy on important telegrams.

The telephone

Inventors and engineers raced to create a way for telegraph wires to carry the human voice. Scottish inventor Alexander Graham Bell was the first to patent one. He called his device 'The Harmonic Telegraph.'

1876

The most valuable patent in history

Alexander Graham Bell had a personal interest in helping the deaf communicate. Both his mother and his wife were deaf, and he worked as a teacher of deaf children. He was experimenting with transmitting speech electrically, and patented a device in 1876 on the same day as one of his many rivals. It is said to be the most valuable patent in history. It was contested by other inventors for many years, but in reality, like almost every modern invention, the telephone was the product of not one inventor, but the combined work of many people.

1880s–1890s

Early telephones

After Bell's invention, telephone networks began to be established. In the 1880s and 1890s, the first telephone exchanges were set up, allowing users to connect with one another through a central switchboard operated by human operators. The networks expanded rapidly, with telegraph wires being repurposed for telephone use, and new lines being laid.

Bell's telephone used a diaphragm that vibrated from sound waves. It converted these waves into an electric current. The electrical current was then sent over a wire to a receiving device that converted it back into sound.

Alexander Graham Bell
(1847–1922)

"Hello. Operator. Number, please". Most telephone exchange operators were female. It was one of the first commercial jobs that women were allowed to have.

In 1891, American inventor Almon Brown Strowger invented the first automatic telephone exchange.

The record industry

In 1877, the American inventor Thomas Edison invented 'the phonograph,' a machine that could record sound and play it back. It was a by-product of his work on the telephone. The sound vibration waveforms were recorded into the surface of a rotating disk called a 'record.' To reproduce the recorded sound, a playback stylus traced the surface and produced sound waves. Until this point, music was usually only played in public—now performances could be brought into people's homes Listening to prerecorded music became a popular hobby in the mid-1890s. Soon, these commercial recordings gave birth to the record industry.

1910s–1930s

Automatic switching

As the number of telephone lines grew, the telephone exchanges became too complex for human operators. In 1915, the first automatic telephone exchange using rotary dial technology was introduced in the United States, enabling users to directly dial numbers. Automatic switching systems began to replace manual ones.

1930s–1950s

Long-distance calls

Long-distance calls were technically challenging. Telephone lines can't just be made longer and given boosters to amplify the sound when it becomes too weak. If this is done, the amplifiers make the background noise louder and after a while it all becomes background noise. Claude Shannon, a mathematician, worked on how to improve this.

In the 1960s, the use of satellites began, paving the way for mobile phones.

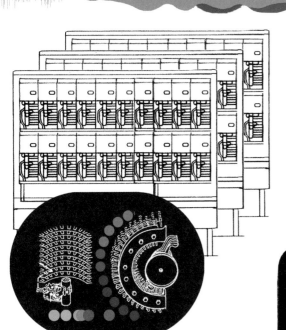

The first transatlantic telephone call was made in 1927 between the United States and England using radio waves.

1948

A Mathematical Theory of Communication

Claude Shannon realized that the most efficient way to send information over a telephone line is when it can be represented in binary form: a zero or a one. This simplest unit of information is a 'bit.' He wrote a paper 'A Mathematical Theory of Communication' in 1948 that introduced his idea. Waveforms could be converted into bits so that they could become digital waveforms. When sent digitally, sounds could be transmitted over long distances with no loss in quality. Shannon's idea forms the basis of all digital communication today. He is remembered as the father of information theory.

Claude Shannon (1916–2001)

1900

Estimated world population: 1.6 billion
Largest cities: 1. London (6.4 million), 2. New York, 3. Paris

TV had a rapid uptake in the US. In 1950 very few people owned a TV, but by 1960, 80 percent of households had one, and were watching an average of 5 hours per day. Because of this, it was mainly the US that pioneered TV, and US shows were exported all around the world.

BROADCAST

"...in saying that the television news show entertains but does not inform, I am saying something far more serious than that we are being deprived of authentic information. I am saying we are losing our sense of what it means to be well informed".

–Neil Postman

The beginnings of radio

Radio waves were discovered in 1888 by Heinrich Hertz. Engineers soon realized these waves could be used to send information wirelessly. This would be particularly useful for ships which until then had no way to communicate. In the 1890s, Nikola Tesla and Guglielmo Marconi obtained the first wireless patents.

1890s–1910s

Naval radio

The US and Britain had the largest navies at this time. They both invested in Marconi's system. But the Japanese were one of the first to put it in action. During the battle of Tsushima in 1905, the Japanese were said to have defeated the Russians largely because they could outmaneuver them using radio. All the major naval powers adopted radio soon after. Commercial radio, however, took longer to take off.

1910s

Commercial wireless telegraphy

By 1912, two companies, Marconi and Telefunken, were the only two commercial wireless operators. The *Titanic* had a 'Marconi room,' with two staff handling wireless messages. The wireless system, however, was a commercial service for wealthy passengers, and not set up to relay shipping warnings. The wireless crew had actually received several iceberg warnings during the day they sank, but they failed to relay them to the captain.

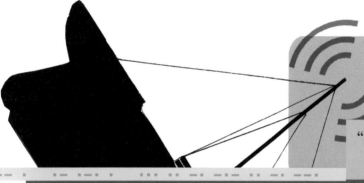

When the Titanic struck an iceberg, S.O.S messages were sent out for help. It was one of the first times the call was ever used. Many heard the call, but frustratingly, not the ships that were closest.

"S.O.S. Calling all stations. This is the *Titanic*. Come at once. We have struck a berg."

1912

The rescue

Another ship, the *Carpathia*, came to the *Titanic's* rescue, but it was three and a half hours away. The 712 people who were eventually saved owed their lives to the wireless. It was a public demonstration of both the power and failings of radio. The Radio Act of 1912 was passed four months later. It made the S.O.S signal the official distress call, and required radio operators to maintain constant radio alert.

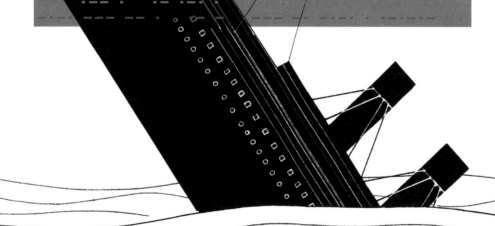

Broadcast

Radio had always been thought of as a two-way communication, like the telephone, and was operated in this way by the navy and large ships. Young teenage hobbyists, however, were fascinated by the technology. They made their own radio receivers and enjoyed listening to faraway ship communications. Radio communication works using two devices—a transmitter and a receiver. A transmitter is very expensive to manufacture, but a receiver can be made quite easily and inexpensively.

This meant something revolutionary: rather than a two-way communication tool, radio could be 'broadcast.' One transmitter could broadcast to thousands of receivers within range. This insight was made by teenagers. In fact, this is not unusual; many innovations in communication began with teenagers. Early computing, the Internet, and social media were all shaped by teenage pioneers playing around with new technology.

1920s

Amateur radio

Teenagers became fascinated with radio. Amateurs built their own receivers to listen in on shipping communication just for fun. Eventually, manufacturers began making radios for the public. Some manufacturers, such as Marconi and Westinghouse, began hosting radio 'shows' as publicity stunts to encourage the sale of their radio sets.

The first radio shows

The first radio shows were very simple. Operators read headlines from the paper or invited music bands to play. Soon, shows came in different formats: music, variety, speeches and sermons, opera, sports, news, weather, and what turned out to be most popular: dramas. The BBC began broadcasting in 1922, and magazines like the *Radio Times* soon followed.

Competition

Radio soon became popular, but radio bandwidth was limited. Only a few stations could operate in an area without causing interference to other signals. This soon turned competitive and amateurs had to compete with professional stations. They either had to turn professional themselves or shut down.

Amos 'n' Andy

The most popular show on early radio in the US was *Amos 'n' Andy*. It featured two white men pretending to be Black characters, and was filled with racist and offensive stereotypes. It began as a nightly show from 1928 and was the most popular show for decades. At the height of its popularity, movie theaters even paused evening film screenings to play the *Amos 'n' Andy* show for the audience. Like other shows, it was sponsored. It continued until 1960.

The first BBC broadcast began with the words "London calling."

1922

1928

Radio in the US

Radio took off fast in the US. At this time, it was a rural country. Weather reports proved invaluable to isolated farming communities. It became enormously popular. The rise of country music is associated with early radio.

Some amateur radio operators on the east coast of the US heard *Titanic*'s S.O.S calls, but could do nothing to help.

91

The radio age

Early radio was very different from how it is now. People sat down and listened with full attention. Talks were more like church sermons than the conversational formats we are used to today. They had a hypnotizing effect. Different formats began to appear: news, sitcoms, music, and sports commentary began to take form.

The Great Depression

In 1929, the US stock market crashed, leading to a period of time known as the Great Depression. Nearly one in four workers were out of work. People had time on their hands, but less money to spend. Radio offered entertainment, so it became very important to many people.

Who pays for the radio?

As the radio industry grew, there was pressure to earn money from the broadcasts. Three different ways of funding radio emerged: state, commercial, and public.

State

In much of mainland Europe the radio was funded by the state, often by the Post Office. This meant it was often free of advertising and commercial pressures, but the state controlled the programming. This model was linked to the rise of far-right governments in the 1930s.

Commercial

In the US, broadcasters provided shows for free. They did this by allowing companies to sponsor and produce the shows—and later by charging companies to advertise. They began selling advertising 'time' in 1922. All kinds of advertisers bought air-time, often hiring popular entertainers to voice their advertising. NBC and CBS emerged as the two big commercial stations.

Public

In Britain, broadcasting was made a public service in 1927 with the setup of the BBC (British Broadcasting Corporation). Australia and Canada followed this model. Anyone with a radio receiver had to pay a license. The BBC used income from the license fee so shows could be independent from advertisers and government. Several other countries also followed this as a model.

Hate speech

Just as early newspapers whipped up public fear, early radio did, too. Speeches, however, are much more emotive than articles. The rise of fascism in Europe was closely linked to radio. And in the US, Charles Coughlin, the 'Radio Priest' gave anti-Semitic sermons to huge audiences. One in four Americans listened to him each week throughout the 1930s, making him one of the most influential figures in the country.

1930s   Mussolini, Hitler, and Coughlin

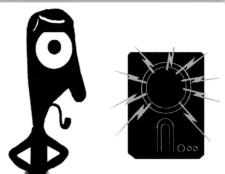

**Franklin D. Roosevelt
(1882–1945)**

The radio president

Until this time, most politicians gave bellowing speeches on the radio as if they were at a rally. President Roosevelt began speaking directly to the public to calm them when there was a fear that banks would collapse during the Great Depression. He explained what was happening with matters of public interest in his 'fireside chats' from 1933 to 1944. Hearing him speak directly to them in a relaxed manner made the public feel a personal connection to their president for the first time. The White House received five or six times as much mail after he began making his radio appearances. Nearly 80 percent of the American public tuned in to listen to his speech after the attack on Pearl Harbor in 1941. This remains the record for a Presidential Address.

Ratings

In the 1940s, a system of ratings was introduced so audience numbers could be counted. This transformed broadcasting. Advertisers paid based on ratings so there was pressure to drive them up. Shows tried to outdo each other to attract bigger audiences. Special-interest shows were canceled in favor of blockbuster shows that would guarantee a large audience.

Transistor radio

In 1956, the transistor radio arrived on the market. Before this, radios were large—around the size of a fridge—and expensive, so there would be only one in a home, which the family would listen to together. Transistor radios were smaller and much cheaper. Teenagers could now own their own radio, and they had very different tastes to their parents' generation.

Soaps

Advertising sponsored and produced many radio shows. The 'soap' dramas are one example. Soaps were dramas aired on weekday afternoons aimed at housewives who were doing housework as they listened. They got their name from the soaps and detergents that sponsored the shows.

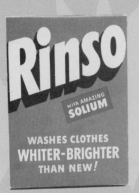

News

The attack on Pearl Harbor in 1941 happened on a Sunday—a day when there were no newspapers. It was a huge national tragedy shared over radio. Once the US entered the war, the public turned to radio for up-to-date news. This marked a turning point where instant news began to weaken the power of the papers.

Youth culture

New radio stations emerged that played music for a younger audience. Rock and roll was born. The youth audiences had money and were seen by advertisers as the consumers of the future. The injection of advertising money gave rise to an entirely new culture based on youth and music. Bands from the US and Britain, the pioneers of radio, became a worldwide phenomenon.

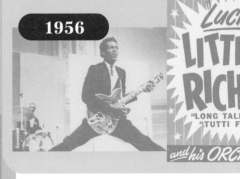

Early radios were large and very expensive.

Transistor radios became the most popular communication device in history. More than 2 billion were sold.

Television

Television was first successfully demonstrated in 1926, and the first broadcasts began a few years later. Programs that existed on radio like soap operas, game shows, and sitcoms quickly moved to television, and it soon became even more popular than radio.

Early TV

In the early days, people watched TV much like we do when we go to the movies today—in silence with the lights off. Shows were created by sponsors who had complete control over the content. The *Texaco Star Theater* was the most-watched show in 1948. Sponsored by Texaco, it began with a dance routine by singing Texaco gas service station attendants. One of the first news programs, the *Camel News Caravan*, was sponsored by a cigarette brand.

Peak attention

In 1950, very few people owned a TV, but within ten years, 80 percent of American homes had one. There were only a few channels, so about half of all households with TVs watched the same shows at the same time—a moment called 'peak attention.' *I Love Lucy* launched in 1951 and became a huge success. The popularity of the show was due to the main character, played by Lucille Ball. It became clear that TV was a medium made for personalities.

Two of the most popular shows in the 1950s were *The Ed Sullivan Show* and *The $64,000 Question*. *The $64,000 Question* and other game shows were later discovered to be rigged.

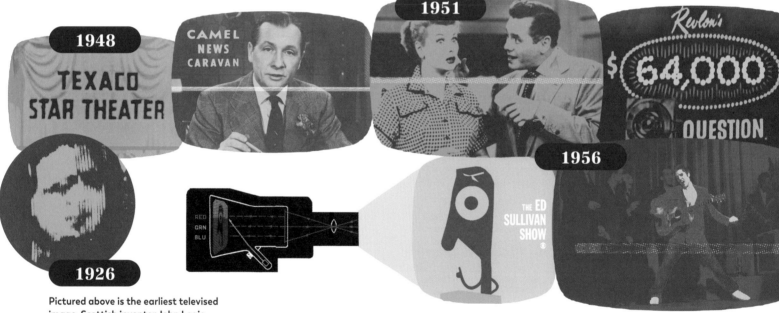

Pictured above is the earliest televised image. Scottish inventor John Logie Baird demonstrated the principle of TV in 1926 with little more than bicycle lights, knitting needles, and a box.

The end of radio?

When TV appeared, people predicted the death of the radio. This did not happen, but the way people listened changed. They no longer gathered to listen together. Instead, people left the radio on in the background while they worked or relaxed. Around this time, the suburbs were expanding and radio became popular to listen to in cars while driving. Shows that required full attention were dropped in favor of short-format talk and music.

The 1950s became known as the decade of conformity, perhaps in part because people were all watching the same TV shows.

The moment of absolute peak attention happened in 1956, when Elvis Presley, already a radio sensation, appeared on TV for the first time. 82.6 percent of Americans tuned in—a record never broken.

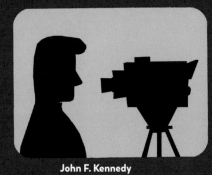

The TV president

In 1960, there was a televised debate between the presidential candidates John F. Kennedy and Richard Nixon. The majority of people who heard the debates on the radio reported that Nixon was the winner, but those that watched the debate on TV favored Kennedy. Kennedy narrowly won, and many attributed the victory to his TV performance. He looked younger and more energetic, and came across as more confident. Commentators said he appeared more 'presidential.' This was one of the first times this word was used. The descriptions were about performance rather than content.

John F. Kennedy (1917–1963)

The new news

TV created yet another era of news. Not everyone read newspapers, but almost everyone watched the news on TV. The Vietnam War was the first war to be televised, and the images the US public saw shocked them.

1955–75

Walter Cronkite was perhaps the most prominent Vietnam War reporter. Despite government attempts to block camera access, the nightly footage of the dead and wounded on TV turned the majority of the country against the war.

Celebrity

With millions of fans, popular media personalities became very influential. Their presence has the power to transform the success of TV stations, films, and magazines. In the TV age, personality itself became very valuable. The screens of the 20th century created icons: Marilyn Monroe, James Dean, Muhammad Ali, The Beatles, and many more.

1967

The Beatles

In 1967, the BBC created *Our World*, the first program to be broadcast all around the world at once. Around 700 million people tuned in—the largest ever audience at that time. The Beatles were asked to record a song to mark the moment. To protest the Vietnam War the Beatles wrote the song *All You Need Is Love* and invited many of the biggest stars of the time to join them.

With more than 290 million album sales, the Beatles are still the bestselling artists of all time. John Lennon in particular had a complex relationship with celebrity. He used his fame to promote peace and social justice issues. But it was fame that ultimately ended his life—he was shot dead by an ex-fan in 1980.

John Lennon (1940-1980)

Through the looking glass

Television quickly became people's main—and often only—source of information. It still has the greatest influence on public opinion today. Its influence shapes everything, from celebrity culture to how politics operates. Everything becomes like a TV show.

Pop culture

In 1941, an ordinary baseball game became a historic TV moment. Before the game, the first ever TV advertisement ran. Advertising turned out to be a much more successful commercial model than sponsorship. TV shows could have more editorial freedom than if they had a single sponsor, and could also make more money. By the late 1950s, this became the dominant model. TV viewing soon became a global activity. American TV shows in particular were exported around the world and shaped popular culture.

First satellite broadcasts

With satellite broadcasts, millions of viewers across the world could view the same events at the same moment. At a time of crisis, such as the assassination of President John F. Kennedy, people gathered around their TV sets across the whole world.

In 1958, 45 million viewers tuned in to watch the NFL Championship Game, in what became known as 'The greatest game ever played.' Its popularity set the stage for the 'Super Bowl.'

1963

1958

1969

The State of the Union address

The State of the Union address is an annual message by the American president that has been delivered in various forms since 1790. It is used to inform the branches of government of the nation's budget, economy, news, and more. However, dry, factual reporting can make a president appear dull on TV. As well as this, the presentation of a controversial policy will get a cold reception from the crowd. None of this looks good for a president. Ronald Reagan changed the format of the address to only present popular content.

1982

The remote control was introduced in the 1950s, but it became widespread in the 1980s. Along with the growing number of channels, it changed the way people watched TV.

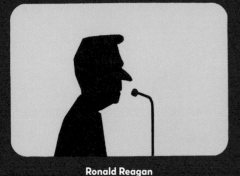

Ronald Reagan
(1911–2004)

The 'likeable' president

In 1980, Ronald Reagan was elected president. In a poll taken after the election, voters were asked why they voted for him. The response was something pollsters had not heard before; they were told he was 'likeable.' Unlike many other politicians, Reagan was comfortable on camera. His background was as a sports announcer and actor. He used techniques unusual for a politician at the time. When he and President Carter were asked to "give voters one final message," Carter replied to the interviewer. Reagan, however, looked straight at the camera and addressed the audience directly. From this moment on, TV presence would carry even more weight than it had before.

The Lenny Skutnik moment

In the 1982 Address, Reagan invited Lenny Skutnik, a government employee who had saved a woman from drowning, on stage. Reagan praised Skutnik as 'American heroism at its finest.' He received a standing ovation, and it was the highlight of the address, giving Reagan a popularity boost. Every year since an American hero has been selected to sit on stage with the president for what has come to be known as the 'Lenny Skutnik moment.'

24-hour news

In 1980, CNN, the first 24-hour news channel, was launched. During times of high drama such as the live OJ Simpson car chase in 1994, the death of Princess Diana in 1997, and the September 11 attacks in 2001, it drew huge audiences. To keep the audience checking back there is pressure to update the story with new content, even if there is no further news. This is known as the 'news cycle.' Other networks, such as Fox and Sky News, launched soon after, and added more sensationalism.

Reality TV

MTV had one of the most lucrative business models of all the channels. They were paid to play music videos, and so had almost no outgoing costs. When the popularity of music videos began fading they wanted to continue to produce cheap shows. In 1992, they launched *The Real World*, a show set in a house shared by people in their 20s. It made for addictive watching, but it became clear it was hard to create drama among reasonable people. More and more provocative guests were cast as time went on.

1980–90s

2000–10s

In 2000, *Big Brother* and *Survivor* were launched. Reality TV soon expanded into every possible area: talent shows, cooking competitions, business deals, and more.

Since 1991, the State of the Union addresses averaged 80 rounds of applause.

Many political events have changed to accommodate TV audiences. Debates, international summits, state visits—everything that is televised can become a political tool to rally support for a government.

Estimated world population: 6.1 billion
Largest cities: 1. Tokyo (30 million), 2. Osaka, 3. Mexico City

All communication has the potential to misrepresent the truth. But in the age of mass media, disinformation has become more powerful than ever before.

DISINFORMATION

"Propaganda is to a democracy what
the bludgeon is to a totalitarian state."

–Noam Chomsky

Propaganda

During the late 19th century, colonization was at its height, and European imperialist powers dominated the globe. Newspaper sales had grown enormously, and the rise of mass media meant mass information. But it also meant mass disinformation. A new field was emerging: propaganda.

Early propaganda

War memorials and imposing military displays have been used since ancient times. Many war memorials were built or named after the battles of Trafalgar and Waterloo in the 19th century—or for Lord Nelson and the Duke of Wellington who led the battles. British cartoons depicted the French Emperor Napoleon as short, when in fact he was average height for his time. But early 19th-century propaganda led to this common myth that persists even today.

Early 1800s

Imperialism

Imperialism was the policy of using military force to extend a country's power and influence. State power and business worked together—armies invaded territories, then export industries were set up. The capitals of Europe became the wealthiest in the world, and Britain became the largest empire of all time—covering a quarter of the Earth's land. To control such a territory, the British Empire required a huge military to be in a state of near constant war. But colonial powers also needed systems of media messaging at home to justify the wars abroad.

Divide and conquer

Ethnic and religious divides were exploited to pit people against each other so they could not unite and overthrow the imperial rulers. Many of today's conflicts stem from these divisions. In colonies such as the US, efforts were made to discourage working class white people from mixing with enslaved people from Africa. If these groups mixed, there would be a higher chance of rebellion.

Press gangs

Until the mid 1800s there was little need for propaganda. If the navy needed men they often just abducted them using 'press gangs.' At the time of the Battle of Trafalgar, over half the British Navy's sailors were 'pressed' men.

Imperial Europe was deeply unequal. While the colonists were very wealthy, working class people were very poor and had few rights.

Some of the most notorious colonial figures: Robert Clive, King Leopold II, Sir Basil Zaharoff, and Cecil Rhodes.

Military technology

Perhaps the main factor driving the Imperial race was technology. The European powers had developed superior military weapons, and could conquer territories with ease. Some battles were won without a single European casualty. The invention of automatic weapons and barbed wire allowed large populations to be contained by very few soldiers, making colonization even more effective. This technological race escalated toward the end of the 19th century.

DISINFORMATION

An extraordinary number of phrases in the english language come from military terms, including 'the blues', 'pipe down', and 'touch and go'.

Racism

Colonization generated huge wealth, so for it to continue, the Indigenous peoples of the colonies were presented in the media as being unable to govern themselves. Stories of ignorance and incompetence, or accusations of crimes were used to legitimize colonization. The racist myth of Europeans as a superior race was used to justify the brutality of slavery and colonization.

Militarization

A huge military was required to control the colonies, so the military was glorified—especially among young boys. Generals were household names, similar to professional athletes today. Lord Robert Baden-Powell and Lord Kitchener were two of the most famous. Their images were printed on collectible cigarette cards.

By 1900, almost half of the world's merchant ships flew the British flag and were protected by the British Navy.

The ideology of racism served the interests of Imperialism. It became so widespread that Jewish people were categorized as a 'race' by the late 1800s. These racist caricatures are too offensive to print here.

Ireland was one of the few colonies where the Indigenous population was white. But like other colonial subjects, they were often portrayed as savages.

The town of Mafeking in South Africa was surrounded during the Boer War, making headlines for months. It was finally liberated, and Robert Baden-Powell, the military leader, became a national hero. He later wrote *Scouting for Boys* which became one of the best-selling books of the 20th century. Its popularity started the Boy Scouts and Girl Guides.

1899

EITHER CONQUER OR DIE

Lord Robert Baden-Powell

CECIL RHODES
CIGARETTES

Gen. Lord Kitchener
CIGARETTES

An army of more than 5 million men protected British colonial interests across the empire. There were 196 different infantry regiments, each with their own uniform, in British India alone.

**Lord Herbert Kitchener
(1850–1916)**

A world at war

In the late 19th century, the rivalry between European powers grew. The race for new territories triggered an arms race. Germany, with an army of 4.5 million, became the world's largest military power. Britain had become vulnerable with a small army of 80,000 troops at home. An alliance was made with France and Russia, but tensions only grew. Europe was going to war. And because Europe controlled the world, it meant the entire world was going to war.

The Great War

During World War I, the British Government coordinated the spread of information in a similar way to how the military campaign itself was run. The 'Ministry for Information' was set up. It is considered the first true propaganda campaign.

The Ministry of Information

Different government departments built support for the war effort. But their messages overlapped and contradicted themselves. The Ministry of Information was eventually set up to coordinate messages. It was headed by Lord Beaverbrook, the most powerful newspaper publisher in the world. London was the world's news and press agency center, which gave Britain a media advantage.

The world's telegraph cables were routed through Britain. One of Britain's first acts of the war was cutting Germany's underwater telegraph cables, effectively silencing their communication with the rest of the world.

Daddy, what did YOU do in the Great

"BE HONEST WITH YOURSELF. BE CERTAIN THAT YOUR SO-CALLED REASON IS NOT A SELFISH EXCUSE"
LORD KITCHENER

ENLIST TO-DAY

54 million recruitment posters were printed in Britain during the war. Many featured Lord Kitchener, the Secretary of State for War.

BRITONS
"WANTS" YOU
JOIN YOUR COUNTRY'S ARMY!
GOD SAVE THE KING

WOMEN OF BRITAIN SAY— "GO!"

Military recruitment

Social pressure was a key to sign-ups in Britain. White feathers, a symbol of cowardice, were given to men on the street who weren't in uniform. And with many men having already made the sacrifice, there was huge pressure on those who had not. Men were often attacked if they had not signed up. In large workplaces such as post offices, workers were recruited together. As were men from towns, villages, clubs, and sports teams. Those

Atrocity propaganda

Appalling false stories were published in the news and the 'Bryce Report' was drawn up by the British Government to document Germany's atrocities. It is credited with helping convince other countries, such as the US, to enter the war. Many of the statements in the report were later found to have been made up

Censorship

Any negative news that might affect morale was censored. A very serious flu pandemic broke out in 1918. Although it is believed to have originated in the US, it became known as the 'Spanish flu' because only Spain, which was neutral, was reporting it.

DISINFORMATION

The 'Hun'

Germans were portrayed as 'The Hun'—barbarians wrecking civilization. By defeating them, the world would be at peace. 'The War to end all Wars' became the slogan throughout the war. They claimed it was necessary to go to war to support peace.

The Committee for Public Information

The US government, copying the British, launched their own campaign to build support for the war. Within one year, the 'Committee for Public Information' had a staff of 150,000.

Drawing the US into the conflict

At the start of the war, the US was a neutral country, and the US public was opposed to involvement in a European war. There was also strong opposition to entering on the side of the British. German-Americans were the largest ancestry group in the US, and did not want to go to war with their home country. However, the British saw the US as crucial to victory and much of their propaganda was aimed at swaying the American public.

Movies

Cinema was a powerful new propaganda tool. Anti-war films were suppressed and pro-war films were encouraged. *The Kaiser*, an American silent film, broke box-office records. It was heavily promoted, and ads declared "All pro-Germans will be admitted free."

Pro-war speeches were regularly given at movie theaters before showings. The speakers became known as 'The Four Minute Men,' because that was believed to be the perfect length of time to deliver a political message.

"If people really knew [the truth] the war would be stopped tomorrow. But of course they don't, and can't know".

– David Lloyd George, British Prime Minister

WWI was the first major war where modern weapons were used on both sides. New technologies such as the airplane, chemical warfare, barbed wire, machine guns, tanks, and grenades were used with awful consequences. Around 20 million people died.

Resentment

There was such anti-German feeling during the war that many German families changed their surnames. Even the British Royal family changed their last name. Their surname was Saxe-Coburg-Gotha until 1917, when it was changed to Windsor. People stopped speaking the German language in the US.

The aftermath

Half of all eligible men in Britain voluntarily enlisted. Governments around the world took notice, and propaganda became a major influence on the rest of the 20th century. One war veteran in Austria wrote with great admiration about British propaganda, arguing it should be simple, repetitive, and aimed at the masses. His name was Adolf Hitler.

Nazism

The total control over the media that Nazi Germany exercised in the 1930s and 1940s was unprecedented. Their atrocities—the deliberate, industrial murder of millions of innocent people—is considered the most depraved act any state has ever committed. How could something like this happen?

Germany in the 1930s

After their defeat in WWI, Germany was punished severely. They were required to give up some of its territory in Europe, all its colonies overseas, and pay billions in retribution. The German economy crashed and a third of men became unemployed. In the dire economic and political turmoil, right-wing parties began gaining support. The people of Germany were searching for answers, and someone to blame.

Magnetic tape

Magnetic tape technology was developed in Germany in the 1930s. Speeches were often recorded and replayed. This was only discovered after the war had ended.

Adolf Hitler

A young right-wing politician, Adolf Hitler, wrote a bestselling book called *Mein Kampf*. It was a manifesto on how he had become increasingly antisemitic and militaristic. He wrote about how propaganda, like advertising needs to first and foremost attract attention, limit itself to a few points and repeat them again and again. Perhaps his greatest insight, however, was his belief that it is more difficult to persuade people logically than stir emotion.

Rallies

In 1919, Hitler gave his first public speech to a crowd at a beer hall. A few months later he was headlining at a rally of 2,000. His speeches followed a similar structure. They began with a silence, which was broken by personal stories of great pain and his despair at Germany's defeat. Then, with rising fury, he would start to blame. In an incredibly intense finish, he would bellow a flood of hatred for Jewish people. The end was a call for renewed greatness and national unity.

The Nazi salute

Enthusiastic audience responses can reinforce a message and whip a crowd into a frenzy. Hitler's close friend was a student at Harvard University, and suggested a chant similar to 'Fight, Harvard, Fight'. This is thought to have been adapted to the infamous 'Sieg, Heil, Sieg', with the 'Heil Hitler' salute at the end. The chants and salutes helped create powerful theatrical effects. His speech, 'Why We Are Anti-Semites' was interrupted 58 times by cheering.

The Aryan race

Hitler was heavily influenced by *The Passing of the Great Race*, a book written by US white supremacist Madison Grant. He referred to this pseudo-scientific book as his 'Bible' and based some of his own book *Mein Kampf* on it. The race Grant was referring to was a mythical 'Nordic race.' The idea of an 'Aryan race' came largely from this.

The swastika

This ancient symbol was found on ceramics in many great civilizations. Hitler choose it as a way to suggest a racial lineage to great civilizations.

Hitler Youth

Scouting was banned in 1933. Instead, youths were encouraged to join the 'Hitler Youth.'

The People's Radio

The German government subsidized the manufacture of a radio so every household could afford one.

"All of Germany listens to the Führer with the People's Radio."

Blame

Jewish people were blamed not only for Germany's problems, but also for the war itself. Like all far-right ideologies, the Nazi's power rested on anger and blame, as seen in propaganda posters like the one below:

"The war is his fault!"

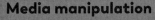

Media manipulation

In 1933, Hitler seized power and created the Ministry for Propaganda. Its head, Joseph Goebbels, focused on scaling up Hitler's speeches to reach the whole population. The key to the campaign was radio. To keep listeners tuned in, it was mainly light musical entertainment mixed with some political material. This, however, led up to a big speech called a 'National Moment'. In this way, Nazi party ideology was injected into the daily life of nearly every German.

The largest audience in history

The radio can be turned off or tuned to another station. The Ministry's answer to this was the 'radio guard.' Party loyalists ensured everyone was tuning in. During the times there was a 'National Moment,' all work would stop and radio guards moved people into special listening rooms. During these moments, Hitler's voice reached an estimated 70 percent of the population: 56 million people—at that time, by far the largest audience in history.

The aftermath

After the Nazis were defeated in WWII, the sickening horror of what had gone on emerged. The word 'propaganda' took on a negative meaning. However, the techniques of persuasion that had been developed during WWII didn't disappear. Far from it. They just found a new market. Rather than serving military objectives, they would instead serve business interests.

Advertising

Advertising has been around since ancient times, but it began to grow enormously in the 19th century. By the 20th century, advertisers began using more sophisticated psychological persuasion techniques, and it grew into one of the world's largest industries.

Early advertisements

The earliest newspaper advertisements were for books; spare print space could advertise other items the printer had for sale. As papers became popular, the most common ads were for 'cure-alls.' In the US, 'snake-oil' ads became infamous. Traveling salesmen had been common in the early 19th century, but after the arrival of mail order, they were able to sell through the press.

Slogans and brands

Rhyme and repetition make brands memorable. Catchy jingles, repeated slogans, and memorable mascots make brands recognizable and stand out from the competition. Early advertising pitched products as necessary, with rational arguments about why the product was good. It is sometimes referred to as 'reason why' advertising. But that changed after WWI.

Creating desire

In the 1920s, after WWI, emotive and psychological techniques began being used. Shame or fear were sometimes instilled, with a product offered as the solution. Adverts would try to link brands with positive emotions like freedom or happiness, even if there was little connection to the product itself. By applying these methods, advertising had effectively discovered a limitless market. Consumer culture was born.

Late 1800s

Dr Simm's Arsenic Complexion Wafers

Snake oil became infamous. Clark Stanley's oil was not only found to have no medicinal benefits, it also contained no actual snake oil.

Cure-all businesses were mostly shut down when laws were passed in 1906.

CLARK STANLEY'S SNAKE OIL LINIMENT

1900s–20s

The BEST is ALWAYS at J.Sainsbury's

Campbells' Soups

The Way to Get Rid of that Cough!

Peps 'A Pine Forest in Every Home.'

Drink Coca-Cola Delicious and Refreshing

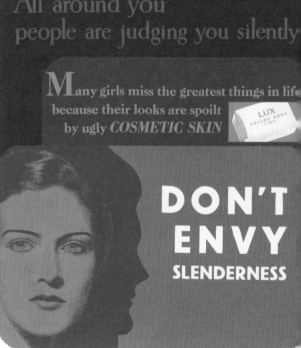

1920s

All around you people are judging you silently

Many girls miss the greatest things in life because their looks are spoilt by ugly COSMETIC SKIN

LUX TOILET SOAP

DON'T ENVY SLENDERNESS

Propaganda

The word advertising comes from 'advertere', which is Latin for 'turn toward.' In several European languages, the word for advertising is 'propaganda.'

BRIGHTER WHITER

IMAGINE LUXURY

Billboards began in the 1830s. Today there are more than 350,000 million in the US alone.

Glamour

Magazines that feature glamorous lifestyles will find it easier to fill advertisement spaces because people are more likely to respond to advertising after reading particular types of articles. Magazines tend to be glossy and glamorous.

The red and white Santa Claus was popularized by Coca Cola in 1931. Before this, he was often in green.

Christmas

Christmas is the most lucrative time of the year for many manufacturers. But where does this festival come from? The tradition of gift giving pre-dates Christianity. The Roman feast of Saturnalia was celebrated by exchanging joke-gifts. Expensive gifts were frowned upon; the lowlier the gift, the stronger the bond of friendship it was said to represent. It was the most popular festival in the Roman calendar. When Rome converted to Christianity, religious leaders could not ban it without a backlash, so the tradition carried over. But it was only in the 20th century that Christmas became the consumer phenomenon it is today. If the audience is thinking about Christmas when they see an advertisement it is more effective, so it is more expensive to advertise in the run-up to Christmas.

Focus groups

George Gallup founded the American Institute of Public Opinion in 1935. His opinion polls sampled groups of different people for both commercial and political uses. During WWII, the effectiveness of propaganda was also being measured with focus groups.

The advertising golden age

From the 1960s to 1980s, TV and magazine advertising was at its height. The tobacco industry was the true pioneer of advertising throughout. The 'Marlboro Man' campaign is said to be the most successful campaign of all time. David Ogilvy became known as one of the greatest copywriters in the industry. He had worked at Gallup, and was known for his careful analysis of the target audience.

Public relations

People began paying less attention to adverts, so rather than paying a magazine to run an advertisement, advertisers looked for ways to pay the magazine to write positive articles about them. Movie producers, too, are paid to show products or convey ideas. This became known as public relations.

1935

AMERICAN INSTITUTE OF PUBLIC OPINION

"At 60 miles an hour the loudest noise in this new Rolls-Royce comes from the electric clock"

1960s–80s

Come to where the flavor is.

Filter cigarettes were seen to be for women when they first appeared. Marlboro depicted a rugged, masculine stereotype to convince men to smoke them. They went from 1 percent of sales to the 4th best-selling brand in the US in a year.

1984

Sponsorship

The 1984 Olympics in Los Angeles pioneered the concept of sponsorship deals. That year received record funding, which paved the way for sponsorship of other major public events. In the same year, the shoe company, Nike, began a landmark sponsorship deal with the famous basketball player Michael Jordan.

Movies

Movies were a very important platform for advertising. And not just for the ad breaks. Many Hollywood actors, from the most famous femme fatales to John Wayne, were paid by tobacco companies to smoke in films.

Public relations

Following WWI, propaganda strategists directed their attention to commercial work. Persuasion could be used not just as a sales tool, but as a way to deflect criticisms, shape public opinion, and even change laws.

The Red Scare

The most wide-reaching public relations campaign in the 20th century was the targeting of trade unions and labor busting. In a campaign known as the 'Red Scare,' a fear of communism was instilled, and prominent figures were accused of sympathising with communism. Campaigns in the US were funded by the Central Intelligence Agency (CIA), while in the UK they were led by the Information Research Department (IRD) and other agencies.

Women smoking

Until the early 20th century there was a taboo against women smoking. Edward Bernays was hired by tobacco company Lucky Strike to change this. His company paid models to stand in front of a suffragette march and smoke. The images of women smoking shocked the public. At the time, young women were yearning for freedom, and the reports linked smoking with liberation. In the years that followed, women began smoking as much as men.

Cars in cities

When cars arrived in cities, so too did road deaths. Public anger was directed at motorists and severe restrictions were proposed in cities. Car manufacturers stepped in to shift blame to pedestrians and campaigned to legally remove them from the road. The term 'jaywalking' was first coined in the PR materials of carmakers. Only later was it made a law.

Single-use packaging

The 'Keep America Beautiful' campaign helped reduce litter by 88 percent across the US. However, this was actually an example of 'astroturfing.' The campaign was covertly paid for by companies from the packaging and drinks industry, including Coca Cola. At the time, these companies were switching from refillable glass to single-use plastic, which was causing litter. The state of Vermont responded by banning single-use packaging. The campaign was set up after this ban because the packagers were worried other states would do the same. Rather than making their businesses sustainable, the campaign shifted responsibility of litter to the public.

1920s

BELIEVE IN YOURSELF!

An Ancient Prejudice Has Been Removed

1929

Before jaywalking laws were introduced, pedestrians had as much right to the roads as cars.

DON'T JAY WALK

WATCH YOUR STEP

1950s

A CLEAN SWEEP

KEEP AMERICA Beautiful

DON'T BE A LITTERBUG

1970s

The Keep America Beautiful campaign made 'litterbug' a household word.

GET INVOLVED NOW. POLLUTION HURTS ALL OF US.

People start pollution. People can stop it.

In 1953, the state of Vermont passed the 'bottle bill', which aimed to ban the sale of non-refillable containers. The Keep America Beautiful campaign began in the same year.

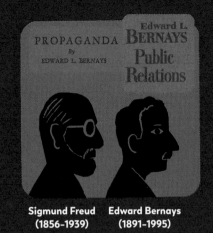

Sigmund Freud (1856–1939)

Edward Bernays (1891–1995)

From propaganda to public relations

The term 'public relations' was coined by Edward Bernays, who worked for the US propaganda unit during WWI. In 1928, he wrote a book on persuasion techniques called *Propaganda*. In 1945, after propaganda had become a negative term, he wrote another book called *Public Relations*. He created many of the most influential advertising campaigns in history. In a campaign to launch the first paper cups he introduced a fear of bacteria for the first time. He popularized the 'substantial' breakfast of bacon and eggs, for a meat company. He even helped remove a government. The United Fruit Company hired him to turn the Guatemalan people against their government. When they successfully removed the government and installed one that would be dictated to by a fruit company, the country became known as a 'Banana Republic.' Bernays was the nephew of the psychologist Sigmund Freud, and applied his uncle's psychoanalysis ideas to public relations. But he also applied his public relations ideas to his uncle by helping to market and popularize Freud and his theories, especially in the US.

Climate denial

When it was first suggested that the fossil fuel industry's CO2 emissions were causing climate change, some in the industry hired the same PR companies as the tobacco industry, and set up groups such as 'The Global Climate Coalition' and 'Information Council for the Environment' to question climate science. At the turn of the 21st century, there was growing awareness about climate change, and pressure was mounting. The PR then changed direction. There was less denial and more greenwashing.

Greenwashing

In the 2000s, oil companies focused heavily on greenwashing. BP launched a campaign to encourage people to reduce their emissions as individuals, when they could instead have focussed those efforts on doing more to improve their own carbon footprint. They were responsible for the largest marine oil spill in history when in 2010, one of their oil rigs, 'Deepwater Horizon', exploded. Despite this, the greenwashing has been a huge success: a marketing poll in the UK showed BP as one of the top 10 'green brands'. They even polled higher than activist group Greenpeace.

1970s–90s

Who told you the earth was warming... Chicken Little?

Let's economize on fuel. Not choice.

✓ COALITION FOR VEHICLE CHOICE

WHO SHOULD CHOOSE YOUR NEXT CAR? YOU OR CONGRESS?

Americans Work Hard For What We Have, Mr. President. Don't Risk Our Economic Future.

A message from members of The Global Climate Coalition

Information Council for the Environment

The Global Climate Coalition

2000s

What on earth is a carbon footprint?

The term 'carbon footprint' was actually coined by BP. BP hired the advertising agency Ogilvy in 2004, which shifted responsibility to consumers.

BP, originally British Petroleum, rebranded itself as 'Beyond Petroleum' in 2000.

"I think it is, in many ways, the most serious crime of the post WWII era, anywhere in the world. The consequences of what they've done are just almost unimaginable... It is the moral equivalent of a war crime."

–Al Gore, Former US Vice President, on the climate denial of the fossil fuel industry

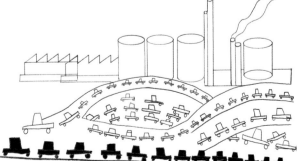

Modern propaganda

It is often claimed that our press is free and can publish whatever it wants, and so its media is free from propaganda. The reality, however, is different. There is always a temptation to mislead, and this is true in all societies and of all forms of government. Wherever there is information, there is disinformation.

How can propaganda operate in a free press?

In the book *Manufacturing Consent*, Edward S. Herman and Noam Chomsky (p9) argue that although in theory there is a free press, in practice, what is published serves big business and government interests. How is this possible? They describe five different ways the press is filtered— through ownership, access, fear, advertising, and flak.

Flak

If a journalist or whistleblower reveals a story that is inconvenient for those in power there can be legal threats, and sometimes changes in the law. There may be moves to discredit them. Their credibility or personal life may be smeared or stories invented to change the conversation. When WikiLeaks (see above-right) began posting damaging videos and documents from the Iraq War, its founder Julian Assange was targeted and imprisoned.

Ownership

Most media companies are big businesses with different clients. Many deals also rely on government contracts. While an individual journalist might want to publish a hard-hitting story, the paper they work for is ultimately a business. A story may not run if it risks losing the company money.

Access

Journalists rely on contact with people in power to get the stories for the news. If they challenge those in power, they will not be given access. On the other hand, if a journalist gives a politician positive coverage, they will likely be granted exclusive stories and more interviews.

Fear

An enemy is very useful as a way to deflect negativity: someone or something to blame and fear. In Nazi Germany it was 'the Jews.' It is often said that without this imagined threat, the Nazis could not have risen to power. The west has had a series of enemies since the end of WWII.

Advertising

The media often relies heavily on advertising. The companies that advertise have interests and business connections. The threat of canceling profitable advertising deals will make the media think twice about running critical stories.

Collateral Damage

Precision Strike

Security Forces

Language

Wording is important to how news events are presented and interpreted. Descriptions of military actions are often worded to appear less severe than they are. However, violence by an enemy is described using emotionally charged language. Even the nonviolent Martin Luther King Jr. was once branded a 'terrorist.'

1964
Vietnam War
Gulf of Tonkin
"US ship attacked off N. Vietnam."

2002	
Iraq War	**"US Says Hussein**
Weapons of Mass Destruction	**Intensifies Quest for**
"Bush Cites Urgent Iraqi Threat."	**A-Bomb Parts."**

While some wars and issues get daily coverage, others go almost completely unreported. What makes the news is decided by editors and media owners.

Making the case for war

Disinformation can be used to manipulate public opinion or escalate conflicts that lead to war. Two of the largest wars of the last 60 years began with disinformation. The Vietnam War was escalated by an alleged attack on a US ship in the Gulf of Tonkin, and Iraq was invaded after the claim that Iraq had been developing weapons of mass destruction. Both of these claims were later proved to be incorrect.

WikiLeaks

WikiLeaks' revelations have been very damaging to the reputations of many governments and corporations around the world, but none more so than the US. Leaks exposed war crimes, cover-ups, and shocking videos of the US military in action. Some leaks showed the US had been spying on people—even important figures. Other leaks revealed that the US military had tried to keep the number of civilian deaths secret. Their records in Iraq show that 15,000 extra civilian deaths were known about but not reported.

Julian Assange (1971–)

The rise of the US Military

After WWII, Europe was in ruins, and the US took over as the world's military superpower. The US spends more on its military than the next nine countries combined. Today, the US Department of Defense is, by many metrics, the largest organization in the world. It employs 2.9 million people. By contrast, the world's largest company, Walmart, has 2.1 million employees, while Amazon has 1.6 million. It operates 750 military bases across 80 countries.

Military technology

Today, the military and technology are closely connected. Huge amounts of funding goes toward the military and much of this is on the development of high-tech systems. Computers, the Internet, GPS, and many other technologies began as US military research that later became available to private firms and consumers. This partnership is sometimes referred to as the 'military industrial complex.' In many ways, it shapes our world today. Let's take a closer look at how some of these technologies were developed.

Hollywood

Films that portray the US military in a positive light can be given subsidies from the Department of Defense. This proved so profitable that by the end of the 1980s movie producers were urging scriptwriters to create military-related plots. *James Bond*, *Air Force One*, *Transformers*, *Top Gun*, and *Black Hawk Down* are among hundreds of movies that were made this way.

The Arms Industry

A single aircraft carrier costs $13 billion, and drones can cost $400 million. Arms manufacturing is very lucrative. Governments are often unable to decrease military spending because the arms industry forms a powerful lobby.

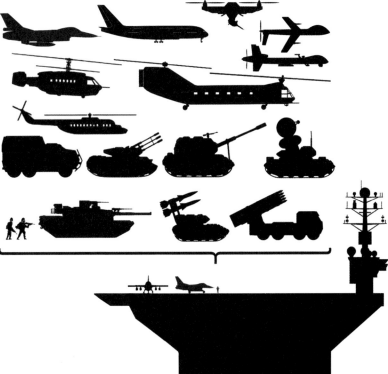

Estimated world population: 8.1 billion
Largest cities: 1. Tokyo (37 million), 2. Delhi, 3. Shanghai

The computers and digital devices we use today are all based on the same concept. Alan Turing, who devised this concept, called it the 'Universal Machine.' Turing is considered the father of computer science as well as Artificial Intelligence. He also codesigned the first computer game, a chess program, in 1948.

COMPUTERS

"This is only a foretaste of what is to come
and a shadow of what is going to be."

—Alan Turing, 1949

How does a computer work?

A computer is a machine that processes information. It adds, it multiplies, and does all sorts of calculations. But how does it do that? How can a machine be made to calculate?

Bits

If we ask a computer to add '1 + 2' it can only react to one simple instruction that says either 'on' or 'off.' This instruction is called a 'bit.' A bit is written as either a 1 or 0 to represent the on or off state.

Bytes

Bits are combined together in groups of eight called 'bytes.' A byte has 256 different possible combinations, which is enough information to hold a letter or number. Colors and other data can be represented by larger groupings of bytes.

Circuits

Using only 1s and 0s, complex instructions can be built that tell the computer what to do. With circuits made up of clever operations called logic gates, bytes can be added together, subtracted, multiplied, and do any number of other mathematical operations.

Programs

The sets of instructions a computer uses are called programs, and they get very complex. By the 1960s, there were programs that had over a million lines of instructions. Although the computer only understands 1s and 0s, the information flows as electricity at close to the speed of light.

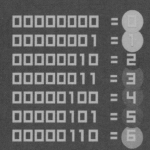

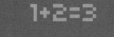

This logic gate is adding the number 1 to 2, and giving the answer of 3.

Speed

The huge advantage that computers have is their mind-boggling speed. The 2017 AI chess master AlphaZero learned to become a chess master in a day. It played 44 million games of chess against itself in 9 hours.

Programming languages

Programming languages are systems used to instruct computers to perform tasks. They serve as a means of communication between humans and machines, allowing programmers to write code in a format that can be understood and executed by a computer. Languages have specific rules and grammar that dictate how code must be written.

Grace Hopper

Grace Hopper was a pioneering computer programmer and inventor. She helped develop the first computer languages, and contributed significantly to the development of COBOL, one of the most widely used programming languages in the world. She is also known for popularizing the term 'computer bug.' In 1947, while trying to fix a computer glitch, her colleague found that an actual bug—a moth—had become stuck, jamming the computer. During Hopper's time, the field was dominated by men. She paved the way for women in technology. However there is still a lot of work to be done today to ensure gender equality in the field.

**Grace Hopper
(1906–1992)**

How does a computer play chess?

The game of chess can be broken down into individual moves, which can be ranked according to how advantageous they are. The total number of possible moves that occur in a game is impossibly large and could never be calculated by a human. But a computer can be programmed to assess every possible move for the next several rounds. From this, it can evaluate the best strategy and move accordingly.

The probability calculation for three moves in chess is approximately 20x20x20, which is a total of 8,000 possible combinations. For six moves, it is approximately 20x20x20x20x20x20, which is 64 million possible combinations.

Processing

Modern computers can process very quickly and very accurately. Today, the fastest computer is the Frontier supercomputer run by the US Department of Energy. It can process 11,000,000,000,000,000,000 operations every second. A million times faster than the average desktop computer.

Displays

Although a computer only works in 1s and 0s, it must convert and display information in a way that is understandable for us humans. It does this by converting its output to colors and characters, which are displayed on a screen for the user to see.

1Kb	= 1000 bytes
1Mb	= 1 million bytes
1Gb	= 1 billion bytes
1Tb	= 1 trillion bytes

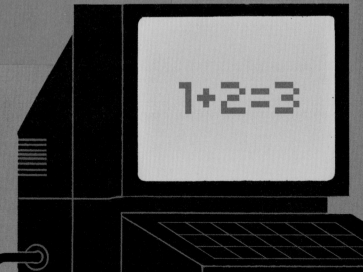

IBM vs Kasparov

Garry Kasparov is said to be one of the greatest chess players who ever lived. But in 1997, he was beaten by the IBM computer Deep Blue. Deep Blue could assess as many as 200 million chess positions per second.

AlphaGo

In 2016, Google's AlphaGo beat world champion Lee Sedol at the strategy game Go. Go has been popular in East Asia for centuries. It is more complex than chess and is often considered more of an art form than a game. Until that time, it was believed a computer could never beat the best human Go players.

Theoretical computing

During the Industrial Revolution, Britain was the center of invention. Every year, new steam-driven machines were being invented to automate more and more things. Charles Babbage, an English mathematician, realized that a machine could be built to automate mathematical calculations.

The Father of Computing

Charles Babbage was in charge of putting together mathematical tables for the navigation and logistic tasks needed to run the British Empire. He realized a machine could be built to perform these calculations, so he devised a machine he called the 'Difference Engine.' He worked on it for 10 years, until he realized that if the machine could feed its own calculations back into itself it could make limitless calculations.

He described this new machine as a 'locomotive that can lay its own railroad,' and called it the 'Analytical Engine.' His design is considered the first modern computer. However, neither the Analytical or Difference were ever built—they required extremely advanced engineering and the budget spiraled out of control. The government withdrew funding, and only a small section was completed.

Although they would have been mechanical, these machines would have operated in much the same way as a digital computer. Instead of a processor, they had a central 'Mill,' and instead of memory they had a 'Store.'

Weaving with numbers

Babbage and his colleague Ada Lovelace were inspired by the Jacquard loom—a machine used to weave patterns in cloth. The engines used punched cards to program complex weaving patterns where each punch-card hole created a part of the design. They realized that rather than designs, these cards could store numbers. Lovelace described the machine as a "loom that wove with numbers."

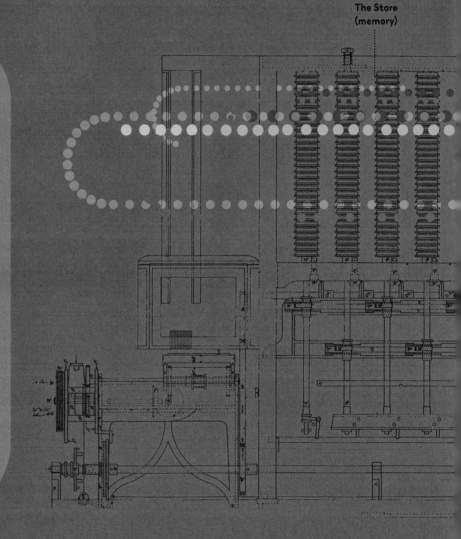

The Store
(memory)

**George Boole
(1815–1864)**

The Laws of Thought

George Boole, another English mathematician, created a system of mathematics using only 0s and 1s. He devised ways to add and subtract these two numbers, binary, using what he called 'logic gates.' These logic gates form the basis of all computer languages. The 'AND' logic gate added one on-off sequence to another. The 'NOT' gate inverts the sequence. A few simple operations—AND, OR, and NOT—are enough, when combined together, to create almost all the complex instructions a computer uses. In 1854, he published his ideas in a book called *The Laws of Thought*.

The mechanisms

When a number was input into the machine, a cog would rotate. When a second number was entered, the numbers could be set to add, multiply, or perform a function through a series of cog and gear turns. This mechanism 'carried' the result up to the next series of cogs, which calculated the next decimal place.

The machine had 50 levels of cogs, so could calculate to 50 decimal places.

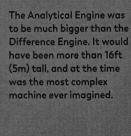

The Analytical Engine was to be much bigger than the Difference Engine. It would have been more than 16ft (5m) tall, and at the time was the most complex machine ever imagined.

The Mill
(processor)

The first computer programmer

Ada Lovelace was a fellow mathematician and friend of Babbage who understood the effect his machine could have on the world, perhaps even more than Babbage himself. She wrote a set of instructions for the Analytical Engine, which are considered the first computer programs. She envisioned how programs could be used to do more than just calculate numbers, and that anything—from images to music to patterns in nature—could be converted into information and one day be manipulated by a computer.

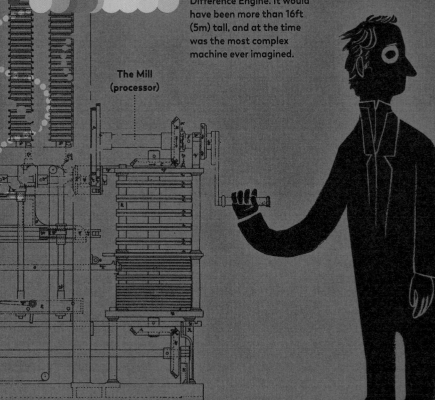

The Difference Engine, 1820s

Charles Babbage (1791–1871)

Ada Lovelace (1815–1852)

Military computing

Many of the world's first computers were developed by the military. Huge investment was made in technology to aim missiles, develop the nuclear bomb, and crack codes.

The need for secrecy

During WWII, radio was used to communicate. But radio messages could be easily intercepted by the enemy. So to keep communication secret, each side encoded their messages. The German codes were extremely sophisticated. Although they could eventually be cracked, it could take months, which was no use because the codes were changed every 24 hours.

Colossus

Mathematicians worked as code breakers. Some code breakers believed it might be possible to build a machine to speed up the calculations. After a huge effort involving many of the most brilliant mathematicians of the time, Colossus, the first electronic, digital, programmable computer, was built in 1943. Its design was inspired by the work of English mathematician Alan Turing, and was built by engineer Tommy Flowers. It could process 5,000 characters per second, and it cracked the German code.

Joan Clarke worked on the math behind cracking the codes. Some historians claim that the cracking of the codes may have shortened the war by as much as two years.

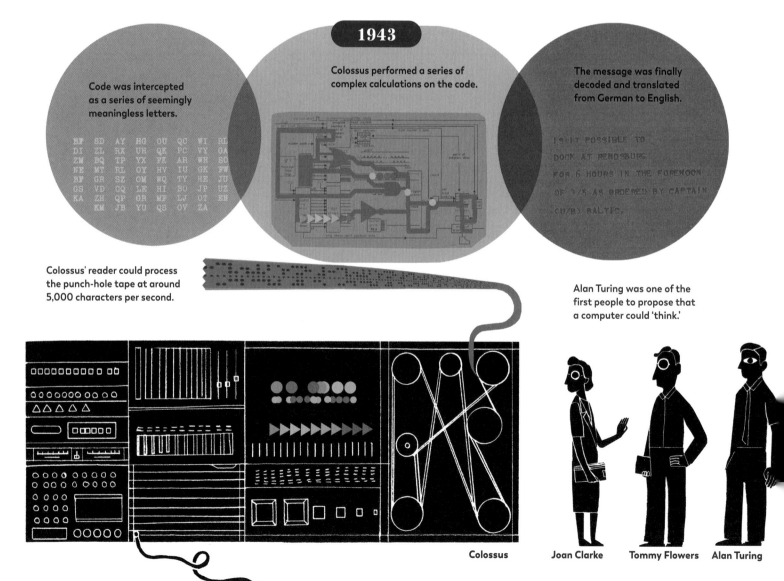

1943

Code was intercepted as a series of seemingly meaningless letters.

Colossus performed a series of complex calculations on the code.

The message was finally decoded and translated from German to English.

IS IT POSSIBLE TO DOCK AT RENDSBURG FOR 6 HOURS IN THE FORENOON OF 3/5 AS ORDERED BY CAPTAIN (U/B) BALTIC.

Colossus' reader could process the punch-hole tape at around 5,000 characters per second.

Alan Turing was one of the first people to propose that a computer could 'think.'

Colossus   Joan Clarke   Tommy Flowers   Alan Turing

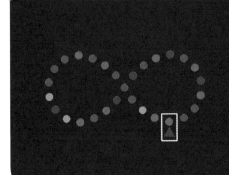

The Automatic Machine

As a student, Alan Turing came up with his idea for what he called 'The Automatic Machine,' or what we now call the Universal Turing Machine. This machine would have a looped tape with a head that would read, and then overwrite, the tape—an operation known as the 'infinite loop.' The design of Turing's machine means we don't need 100 computers for 100 tasks; we only need one computer and 100 programs. Today, almost all computers operate in this way.

The price of secrecy

Although Colossus was far ahead of its time, it had little impact on the development of computing. The British government kept the project a secret after the war so they could spy on Soviet Russia, who began using the German code system. None of the staff involved in the project were permitted to discuss it. Tommy Flowers tried to create a computer for peace time, and applied for a loan from the Bank of England, but was denied because the bank did not believe such a machine could work. He could not argue that he had in fact designed and built these machines already because his work was covered by the Official Secrets Act.

Had the British developed this technology openly and welcomed private investment, it is quite possible that the center of the computing industry would today be in Britain, and not the US.

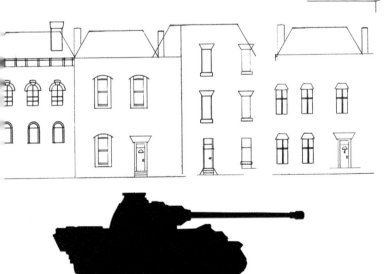

From WWII onward, the US government put unprecedented funding toward computer and military technology.

1944

Harvard Mark I

The Harvard was created to work on the huge number of calculations needed to build the atomic bomb. It was not fully electric, and had mechanical parts.

1945

ENIAC

The Electronic Numerical Integrator Computer was used to calculate the ballistics for different weapons under different conditions. In contrast to Colossus, it was later made public and became widely known. It was hailed in the press as the 'Electronic Brain,' creating a surge in investment in computing.

1950s–1980s

SAGE computer system

During the Cold War, the US made huge investments in technology through a government plan called SAGE. SAGE is still the largest and most expensive computer project in history. It fostered a strong relationship between academic research, the military, and private industry. Among other things, it led to the ARPANET—the first version of the Internet.

Business computing

The earliest computers were developed by governments, but businesses soon saw their potential. Companies such as banks needed to keep track of huge numbers of transactions every day with total accuracy. Computers and machine reading could process transactions and data faster and more accurately.

Machine reading

In the late 19th century, immigration to the US was at its height, and the census department was unable to keep up with the counting. Mathematician Herman Hollerith proposed a solution—a machine that could read. Information was punched as holes into cards where different positions could be used to represent names, jobs, marital statuses, and more. The information contained on the card could be read and recorded in a fraction of a second, and Hollerith's machine was seven times faster at processing the census information than could be done by hand. Hollerith's card reading method proved to be very useful for governments and large businesses. In 1896, he founded a company, which later became IBM (International Business Machines).

1890

On the bottom right we can see the boxes to check where this person comes from.

A punch card was created for each person on the census. The card was inserted into the machine reader, where the metal prongs would go through the card's holes. If a hole is cut, contact is made and the reader counts the data.

1930s–1940s

The most infamous use of punch cards came from Nazi Germany. Identifying and arresting millions of Jewish and Romani people using the census was a huge logistical task. Every concentration camp had an IBM machine and operator. The cards recorded ethnicity, addresses, and the fate of millions of people.

One terrifying Nazi-era poster even declared, "See everything with punch cards."

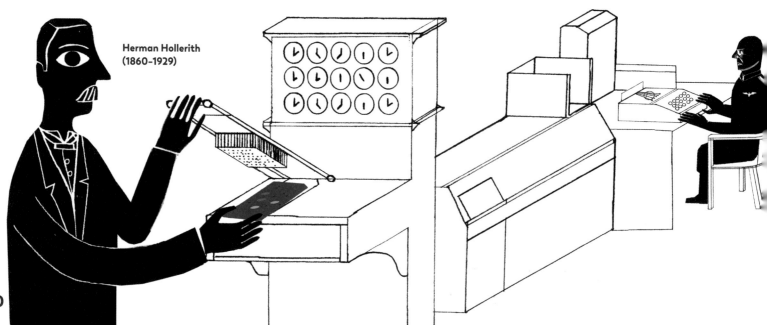

Herman Hollerith
(1860–1929)

Storage

Cardboard punch cards continued being used as storage into the late 1970s, but from the 1950s they began to be replaced by magnetic tape, floppy disks, CDs, DVDs, and hard disks. In 2006, the first cloud storage appeared.

1890s

1950s

1970s

1980s

1990s

The IBM 360

IBM became the leading manufacturer of computers in the 20th century. Their early machines were incompatible with each other, but the IBM 360, launched in 1964, was different. It could be used for various functions. This also meant it could be shared by different organizations, making it cost efficient. It became a huge success, and its new way of operating helped pave the way for the software industry.

Barcodes

In the 1960s and 1970s, supermarkets were growing in popularity, but there were long lines at checkouts since prices needed to be typed in by hand. The barcode was introduced to speed things up. At first, individual stores had to add their own barcodes, but in 1973 manufacturers were persuaded to print the 'Universal Product Code' directly. Barcodes are now almost universally adopted around the world.

Specialist tasks

Early business computers were large, expensive, and did only very specific tasks. Only large businesses could afford them. As they became cheaper, smaller businesses began using them.

1964

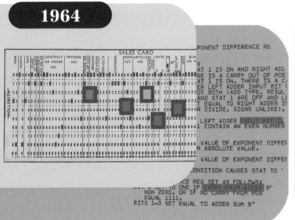

1973

Optical reading

The barcode was inspired by Morse code, and it operates with a similar principle—a sequence of lines of different widths, each representing a digit or character.

A barcode is read by an optical reader. A simple computer operation then retrieves the sale price and prints a receipt.

Personal computing

As computers became faster and more reliable, more businesses began to use them and they began to attract hobbyists. They continued to become more and more affordable, but were still difficult to operate. But when the user interface was improved, they really exploded onto the scene and became a tool for everyone.

1977

First personal computers

The Apple II was the first commercially successful personal computer. Unlike other computers, it came with a keyboard, color graphics, and sound. Its programs were also a big part of its success. The spreadsheet program VisiCalc, and word processor program Apple Writer were easy to use. Apple had found a way to turn a business machine into a personal one. The key to Apple's success was the user interface. Previous computers could only be controlled by writing text commands, but a pointing device (mouse) and icons were much easier for users.

This 'WIMP' system (window, icon, menu, pointing device) is central to user interfaces today.

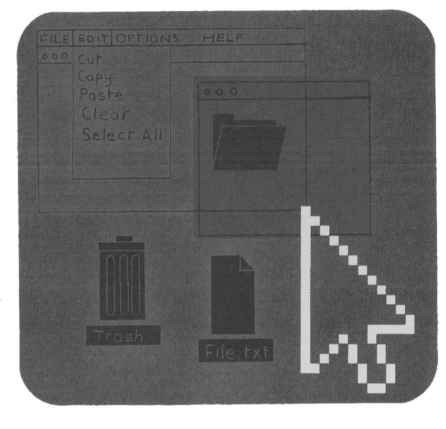

The Homebrew Computer Club

Many computer pioneers including Apple's founders, Steve Wozniak and Steve Jobs, were members of the 'Homebrew Computer Club.' The club had a newsletter and met every month to share designs and ideas in a small San Francisco suburb called Menlo Park. The club soon became the world center for computer hobbyists. When silicon chips made computing cheaper, the industry suddenly became a goldmine. Today this area is better known as Silicon Valley, and is home to many of today's most valuable tech companies.

Steve Wozniak
(1950-)

Steve Jobs
(1955-2011)

The mouse

The American inventor Douglas Englebart developed the mouse and graphical interface. His work was based on how young children learn. Apple was the first computer company to introduce these features commercially.

Steve Jobs described computers as a "bicycle for our minds—a tool to propel and further our mental abilities."

Wi-Fi and Bluetooth

One of the most extraordinary invention stories is that of Hedy Lamarr. She was one of the most celebrated actors in Hollywood, but in her spare time was an amateur inventor. In the 1940s she patented a method of frequency hopping that today forms the basis of Bluetooth, GPS, and Wi-Fi technology.

Hedy Lamarr (1914–2000)

The software revolution

A wave of different software programs became available in the 1980s and 1990s. Excel, Microsoft Word, Photoshop, and others made home computers an essential tool. In 1995, the Windows 95 operating system launched and became an instant hit. Its creator, Bill Gates, became the world's richest man.

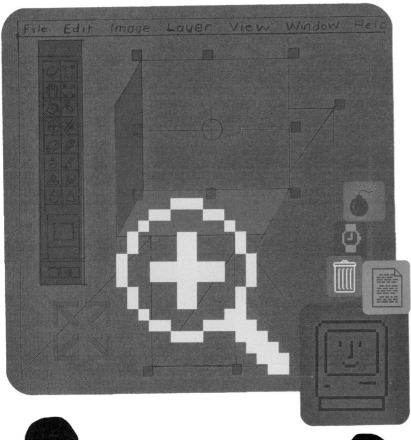

Many industries, from accounting to architecture, publishing, film editing, and music were forever changed by the introduction of computers.

Bill Gates (1955–)

Susan Kare (1954–)

Susan Kare designed many well-known icons for Apple, Microsoft, and later Facebook.

2007

The iPhone

30 years after the launch of the Apple II, Apple reinvented computing again with the iPhone. Unlike other smartphones at the time, the iPhone was built around the device's touchscreen. This gave the iPhone the flexibility to use all kinds of different applications. Developers created applications, or 'apps,' for anything and everything, from weather forecasts to language learning. All smartphones and tablets are now based on this same design.

A touchscreen allows scrolling, swiping, pinching, and rotating, which is very intuitive for a user.

Steve Jobs (again)

The Internet

Different computers used to run on different software and were incompatible with each other. There became a need to connect them together. Allowing them to talk to each other led to more and more developments, paving the way for an entirely new form of communication.

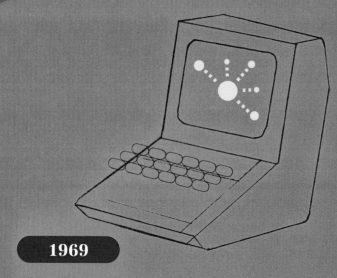

To:
ray.tomlinson@darpa.mil
Subject:
QWERTYUIOP

Today, more than 350 billion emails are sent every day.

1971

Email

When asked what the first email said, Ray Tomlinson, its inventor, replied "it was something like QWERTYUIOP." Then, when he showed his colleagues, he reportedly said "Don't tell anyone! This isn't what we're supposed to be working on." Email soon became the breakthrough 'killer app' of the early Internet. It became hugely popular, and in a short space of time most of the traffic on the Internet was email.

1969

The ARPANET

The predecessor of the Internet, the 'ARPANET,' was created by the US government. Nuclear war was seen as a threat, and they wanted to connect distant computers and create a 'distributed' communication system so if part of the system was destroyed, another could take over. The ARPANET network was later recognized for having educational potential and made available to higher education. It officially became the 'Internet' when the software was updated in 1983.

https://www

1989

The World Wide Web

Tim Berners-Lee, a computer scientist at CERN, a European research facility, imagined a system that would allow the sharing of information. He was partly inspired by a book called *Enquire Within Upon Everything*, which allowed the reader to look up all sorts of questions. He imagined something similar to an index that could locate the same words across different web pages. He built a computer program where these 'links' could be navigated. This new 'space,' 'cyberspace,' became the World Wide Web.

I'm the creeper. Catch me if you can

1969

The first computer virus

The first virus, the 'Creeper Worm,' was designed to travel from computer to computer displaying a simple 'catch me if you can' message. Later viruses were less friendly. The 'ILOVEYOU' virus in 2000 was designed to snatch passwords to give its 24-year-old creator free Internet access. But it went out of control and infected 10 million computers. In 2008, the 'Torpig' virus stole half a million sets of bank details.

As We May Think

Vannevar Bush, a prominent American inventor and scientist, noticed that science papers would often disappear into archives and be forgotten. This meant that researchers were often unaware of other relevant scientific research. In an essay called *As We May Think*, he proposed a system called 'Memex.' Its name was short for a human 'memory extension.' Data would be printed on tiny cards to reduce storage space, and a viewing system would then retrieve the cards on command so viewers could read them with a microscope. The viewing system would allow viewers to make notes and links between the information cards so that future viewers could more easily find them. His system was never built, but the idea closely resembles many of the features of today's Internet.

Vannevar Bush also led the development of the atomic bomb during WWII.

Web-logs or 'blogs' as they came to be known, became popular toward the end of the 1990s.

1993

The first web browser

Mosaic was a program that allowed more user-friendly access to the web. It was called a browser, and it allowed images to be displayed on a 'web page.' This opened the floodgates—the Internet as we know it had arrived.

1995

Amazon

Amazon was one of the first commercial businesses on the web. It began as a bookstore, but now sells almost everything. Online businesses do not have the expense of paying rent and wages so their prices undercut physical stores. This gave people an unlimited variety of goods, but it also changed cities and towns. In just over 20 years, Amazon grew from a garage to one of the most valuable companies on Earth.

1999

File sharing

File-sharing services such as Napster allowed users to share and download music for free, transforming the music industry and sparking huge legal battles.

2001

Wikipedia

Encyclopedias were huge projects which took decades and often involved hundreds or thousands of experts. Nobody could have imagined that within less than a decade a noncommercial project, edited mostly by volunteers and written through trust and consensus, would make most commercial encyclopedias redundant.

1997

Google

The results that search engines (programs that look for things on the web) show were very limited until Google arrived. Google's breakthrough was its indexing method, called the 'page-rank' system. Google's bots count all the links to each website. The website with the most high-profile links is ranked first. Within a few years, 'google' had become a verb.

2000

AOL TimeWarner

The largest Internet provider in the US joined with media giant Time Warner in one of the world's largest-ever corporate mergers. AOL TimeWarner was believed to be invincible. It held the dominant position in almost every type of media, including music, publishing, news, entertainment, and the Internet. However, the executives had misunderstood the nature of the Internet. The corporation imploded two years later reporting a quarterly loss of $54 billion—the largest in US history.

1995

eBay

The online auction site, eBay, began as a hobby for Iranian-American computer programmer Pierre Omidyar. He took no payment on transactions until the high number of users forced him to start making money. It became hugely popular, especially among collectors.

Mobile

Social media became popular in the early 2000s, but when cell phones appeared their use began to accelerate. In 2007, the iPhone was launched, allowing third party applications or 'apps' to run on the device. Other smartphones followed suit. With constant internet access, maps, and cameras, mobile phones began to reshape communication and access to information.

Web 2.0

The precursors of the social media giants we know today began as tiny platforms. Derived from the chat function of online gaming, they were used almost solely by teenagers. The first true social media platforms, Friendster and MySpace, paved the way for what was to come.

Phones are continuously communicating with at least three satellites. They also have a clock so precise that they can detect within a few billionths of a second.

2004
Facebook
'The Facebook' began as an invitation-only social network created by students at Harvard University. Today it has become the world's largest social network, with 3 billion users.

2005
YouTube
YouTube started with home videos, especially of cats. But it grew hugely from 2007 when professional content began to be uploaded. Today, more than 5 billion videos are viewed per day.

GPS

GPS provides useful functions for many apps. For it to be able to work, phones need to communicate continuously with three separate satellites in space. Each satellite is at a known location and sends out radio signals. Although these signals travel extremely fast, there is still a detectable delay. This tiny, billionth-of-a-second delay is what phones use to calculate the distance from the satellite. It knows how far away the satellite is to within a few yards. Using three satellites allows it to figure out your exact position.

GPS (global positioning system) was first used in the Gulf War in 1991. The war took place in a desert, so a navigation system was essential.

2006
Twitter/X
X, formerly known as Twitter, grew massively when celebrities began to use it. Their tweets were often reported in the news, driving more and more visitors to the site.

2007
Maps

2008
Airbnb

2009
Uber

2009
Whatsapp

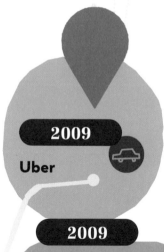

Where r u?

Memes

Just like genes, memes reproduce with variations and mutations.

British biologist Richard Dawkins coined the term 'meme' as a way to describe the viral elements of human culture. Just as reproducing genes create viruses and other biological organisms within chemistry, he argued, memes are the self-replicating ideas and jokes that arise within human culture. The term began to apply to the rapid copying and spread of images and videos across the Internet.

Cameras

Perhaps more than anything else, it was cameras that gave mobile phones their greatest impact on society. On one hand, they have helped expose injustices and amplify marginalized voices, but on the other, they given even more exposure to consumer culture.

2010
Instagram

Instagram was one of the first major apps based entirely on the camera. It launched with filters that masked the poor quality of early smartphone photos. The filters were popular as they made photos and people look attractive.

Less than two years after launch, Instagram was bought by Facebook for $1 billion. Today it has a revenue of $86 billion.

2011
Snapchat

Snapchat became known for its filters. Animated effects such as bunny ears and face swaps were added to live video. Its messages disappear, making them feel more spontaneous.

2012
Tinder

Tinder became the most popular mobile dating app when it launched in 2012. In just a few years dating via phone apps became the most common way to meet a partner.

2016
TikTok

TikTok first launched in China, and expanded internationally two years later. Its success is due to its algorithm that recommends content based on viewing history.

Early smartphone photo quality was so poor it was almost unusable. But camera technology has developed very rapidly.

#nofilter

#BlackLivesMatter
#ArabSpring
#Metoo
#ceasefirenow
2010 2013 2017 2023

The word 'selfie' was declared the Oxford dictionary word of the year in 2013.

Influencers
Popular figures on social media began receiving payments in return for product endorsements. They became known as 'influencers.' Beyonce, Ronaldo, and the Kardashians are some of the best-known figures.

Hashtags
Social media posts sparked discussions. Hashtags were used to find conversations. The use of social media platforms more than doubled in Arab countries during the #Arabspring in 2010. Social media posts revealed the suffering caused by the bombing of Gaza #CeasefireNow.

Going viral

Rather than being a place to share photos with immediate friends, social media platforms began racing each other to enhance engagement. By 2009, posts were spreading more and more widely—they were 'going viral.' The most popular posts could be seen hundreds of millions of times in a matter of hours.

2006
The News Feed

At first, Facebook had a profile page with a 'wall' that others could post on. The News Feed launched in 2006. Continuously changing live updates encouraged users to keep checking back in, driving more engagement.

2009
Likes and shares

'Like' buttons first appeared on the video site Vimeo in 2005, and were introduced to Facebook in 2009. Twitter's retweet button was also introduced the same year. Reposting and sharing soon took over social media.

2011
Algorithms

Algorithmic news feeds are introduced, which means content users previously liked is prioritized. "If you like this, you'll also like that." This means three things: controversial content gets seen more, there are more viral videos (especially cats), and every person sees a different feed.

Even more cat videos
If a person likes a video with cats, an algorithmic news feed shows them more cat videos. If they continue to engage, their feed will become all cats. In this way it is said to 'reinforce patterns of behavior.'

Gatekeepers

In the past, media 'gatekeepers' set our content. On radio, DJs chose the music, and in the film industry producers chose which movies to make. Today, the networks themselves also act as gatekeepers, which makes their owners very powerful.

Collaborative filtering
If a post is liked by many users, the algorithm will prioritize it for other users. This process is known as 'collaborative filtering.' Content that has been tried and tested means that the most engaging content is shown.

Controversies

If a user has negative behavioral patterns, an algorithmic feed can make them worse. Posts that trigger negative emotions such as anger will receive high engagement, making them become more viral. The algorithm then shows users who engage even more infuriating posts. In this way, social media amplifies controversies.

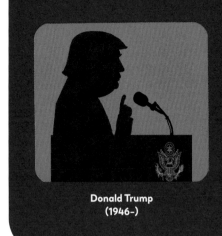

**Donald Trump
(1946–)**

The 'unlikable' president

In the age of TV, 'likability' was a key for election success. But in the age of social media, being unlikable can be more useful than being likable because a controversial figure gets far more attention than an uncontroversial one. In the lead-up to the 2016 election, businessman and reality TV star Donald Trump was quick to recognize this. On social media he ran circles around his political opponent, Hillary Clinton. His angry and provocative tweets were retweeted four times as much as Clinton's. Many in the establishment ridiculed him, but this only made him more combative and even more popular. Combative figures who display hostility toward those in power become popular at times when voters are disillusioned with politics. With the rising influence of money on the political system, it could be said that they are right to be angry.

Trolls

Online, innocent conversations often turn abusive. However, research has shown the majority of people do not become more aggressive when they engage online. The problem is due to a small minority. This minority, known as 'trolls,' seek to deliberately upset others. They often post anonymously, and are almost always men.

Twitter/X

It has been shown that X, formerly Twitter, has the most negative language of all platforms. It is also the most viral. Many celebrities have made use of the platform, but perhaps none so prolifically as President Donald Trump. He tweeted more than 57,000 times. Known throughout his presidency for his controversial tweets, he was ultimately suspended from the platform.

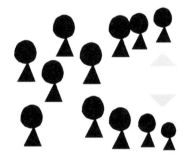

Polarization

Before the 21st century, people watched the same news sources and were getting similar sources of information. When the Internet became our main source of news, political views began to diverge. The more our political debate moves online, the more this happens. It is said to become 'polarized.'

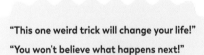

"This one weird trick will change your life!"

"You won't believe what happens next!"

Social media and politics

Social media use has been linked to the rise in nationalist and populist movements all over the world. Both the Trump and Brexit campaigns were heavily promoted through Facebook, while the Bolsonaro campaign in Brazil used WhatsApp.

Clickbait

With endlessly updating feeds, social media became not a place to engage, but to scroll. New forms of media emerged: short viral videos, attention-grabbing headlines, celebrity gossip, and listicles.

Echo chambers

People gravitate toward others they agree with. Over time this drives people into echo chambers which reflect only their own opinion back to them.

Big data

In 2000, Google launched 'AdWords,' an advertising model that used personal data to match sellers to searches. It was extraordinarily effective. Google's profits skyrocketed, making it one of the world's most valuable companies. Others copied their model. This marked the beginning of a whole new economy. One that was based not on real-world things, but on information.

Data harvesting

Advertising and political messaging can be far more effective if the target audience's desires and fears are known. Through searches, friends, comments, and location data, companies can know what people's preferences and concerns are. This information can be very useful to marketing companies.

Data analyzing

By analyzing our personal data in connection with behavioral science, people's personality types can be identified and then categorized into different groupings that are useful to different advertisers. This is especially useful for political targetting.

Microtargeting

Messaging has always targeted specific audiences, but new tech allows this to be done very precisely. For example, political campaigners don't want to target the entire population as many people will not change their votes based on an advertisement. Instead, they target the small number of people who can be persuaded. With data analysis, these 'persuadables' can be identified, and their concerns understood.

Analyzing behavior

Data analysis makes it possible to see which images will likely catch a person's attention and which buttons they are most likely to click. The words they use, the videos they share, how fast they type, and spelling errors all reveal useful information.

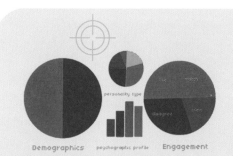

Demographics   psychographic profile   Engagement

Tailoring the message

Customized advertments and videos can be made to target small groups differently on the very same issue. For example, people who are identified as responding to fearful messaging may be shown one image, while a second group who respond to warm messaging are shown a different one.

All time activity: Comments 10,056   Likes 25,704   Friends 526

Data points

With just a few likes or follows a social media company can begin to build a picture of who a person is. They can, for example, guess a person's likely voting preference. Each of these likes or follows is a 'data point.' It has been shown in tests that computers can predict someone's behavior better than their spouse or closest friend.

Cambridge Analytica

Cambridge Analytica was a data analysis company that specialized in political campaigns. They became famous in 2016 after working on the Brexit and Trump campaigns. They claimed to have 5,000 data points on every single voter in America.

One of the keys to harvesting data is the use of 'cookies.' These latch on to a user and send the data back to websites.

XKeyscore can track an individual's online history and listen via their mic, even if the device is turned off.

Edward Snowden (1983–)

Global surveillance

Since 2001, the NSA (the US National Security Agency) has had the capability to gather data on civilians worldwide. They cooperate closely with tech companies as well as network providers and others. Their international network can collect the content of emails, phone calls, Internet searches, and more. Their software, XKeyscore, gives the ability to track anyone in the world, including watching their live browsing, and hijacking access to their microphone and camera. This data gives governments a greater surveillance ability than any state has ever had. If there is ever a move toward authoritarianism there is little we can do. It is hard to overstate this risk. These powers that have the potential to undermine our democracy were never debated or even known about by the public until they were leaked by whistleblower Edward Snowden.

Real-time responses

Advertisers can see when their ads are watched and at what point people stop watching. Different versions are often sent out at the same time. The version that is least effective is removed, and new versions are created and measured again. This technique is known as 'A/B testing.' By using techniques like this, all sorts of online content can be made more effective.

Who is listening?

While technology companies can access data on us, we know next to nothing about how they operate. Some people have long suspected their devices are listening to their conversations. Although the companies deny this, there is no way to be sure. In 2019, it was discovered that some models of the Google home security device, Nest Secure, had a microphone embedded in it, which was not mentioned in the technical specs. When confronted about the fact it was not listed, Google said it was never used, and its omission from the specs was an error.

View post?
Watch video?
Like?
Share?
Disagree?

Likes and shares are fed back instantly. This is useful during election campaigns when news changes so quickly.

Our pocket data-collectors
Google developed the Android mobile operating system in 2007 and released it for free. The only thing they sought in return was the ability to collect user information. By 2011, it had become the world's most popular mobile operating system. Over 3 billion active users feed user data back to Google every day.

The power of big data

In one famous case, a supermarket chain knew a woman was pregnant before she did. She had switched shampoos to less scented products. A dislike of strong scents is known to be an indicator of pregnancy, so targeted baby product ads were sent to her household, alerting them before she was ready to share the news.

Pokémon Go

The game *Pokémon Go* was developed by a company that began as an internal start-up within Google. When the game launched, advertisers paid to bring users close to their shops. It generated billions in revenue.

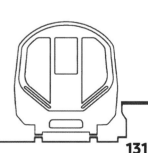

Big Tech

Today, most of the world's information is controlled by a handful of giant technology companies. Known as 'Big Tech,' they are almost all of today's most valuable companies. It is the same pattern seen throughout history. Those that control information, control society. But why is that? What exactly is information?

Control and information

In 1948, the American mathematician Norbert Wiener published a book called *Cybernetics*. It isn't well-known today, but was very influential at the time, and was a key idea in the early development of what became the field of Artificial Intelligence. In the book, Wiener proposed that information is actually a means of control. He described how information controls all sorts of systems including humans, animals, and machines.

Human and animal control

Humans and animals have brains that gather data from the sense organs and process it. We use our brains to identify dangers and goals in our environment and respond to them with an action. If a target is on the right, we move right; if we move too far right, then we correct our action with a movement to the left. This mechanism is repeated until a goal is reached. We are displaying a behavior. The brain controls the body based on the information it is receiving.

Machine control

Machines also gather and process data. These systems can be complex, but in essence it is a simple principle. A thermostat, for example, is the simplest data-processing device. It has two actions: on and off. Two target temperatures are set—when the device detects one temperature it turns the heat off, and when it detects another lower temperature it turns the heat on. In this way, it can be said to process information. Information systems can be thought of as control systems, and control systems as information systems.

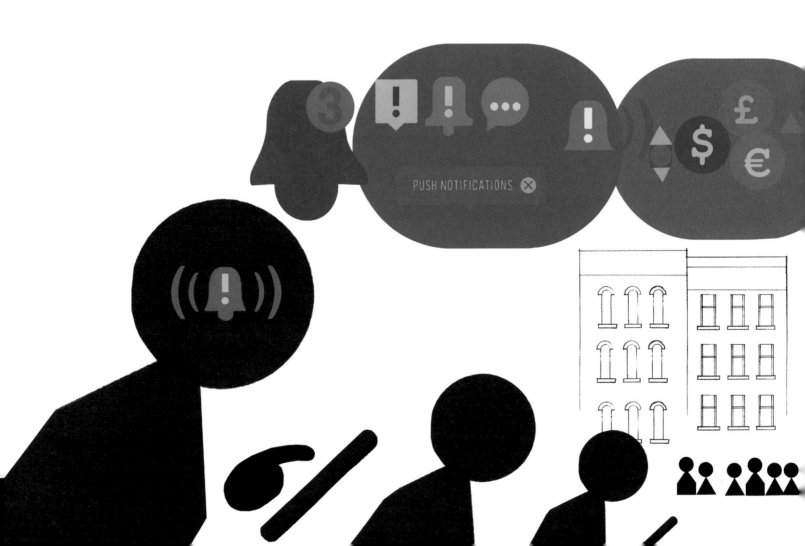

A child genius

Norbert Wiener was world famous as a child for being an extraordinarily gifted student. He was awarded his first degree in mathematics at age 14. He then went on to study zoology and philosophy before completing a math PhD at Harvard University by age 19. The following year, he traveled to England to work with renowned mathematician Bertrand Russell to study the rules of logic. Mathematical logic contains many paradoxes (things that contradict each other), such as 'This sentence is false.' Was there a way to remove them? They worked on this for years, but were unable to make progress. Later, another young mathematician, Kurt Gödel, shocked the world when he showed that paradoxes were in fact impossible to remove. Logic itself, is, in the end, illogical.

Norbert Wiener (1894–1964)

CYBERNETICS
OR CONTROL AND COMMUNICATION IN THE ANIMAL AND THE MACHINE
Norbert Wiener

Cybernetics: the science of control

In his book, Norbert Wiener coined the word 'cyber.' He used an ancient Greek term, which is the root of our word for governor. The Greeks had used it to mean both 'steering rudder' and also 'government.' Wiener chose this term to show that cybernetic systems govern not just animal and machine behavior, but all of nature, as well as economics and society. Toward the end of his life, Wiener was highly critical of scientific research by the military and refused all funding. He wrote articles calling on fellow scientists to do the same.

Big Tech

Today if we want to look for information, we search. Each time we do, we are training algorithms to know more and more about what we want. The data that is collected improves the services for us, but it is not the primary aim—no money is generated from this. Tech companies earn their money from advertising. The results they show us, and the interactions we engage with online, are biased. We may train the algorithm, but the algorithm also trains us. It is this that has made Big Tech the richest companies on Earth. Their wealth is generated by clicks that lead to purchases. But these consumption habits come with a cost.

Inequality

Today, just eight men own the same wealth as the 3.6 billion people who make up the world's poorest half of humanity. The 'Gini Coefficient', which measures inequality, is a complex issue, but has generally been increasing since 1800.

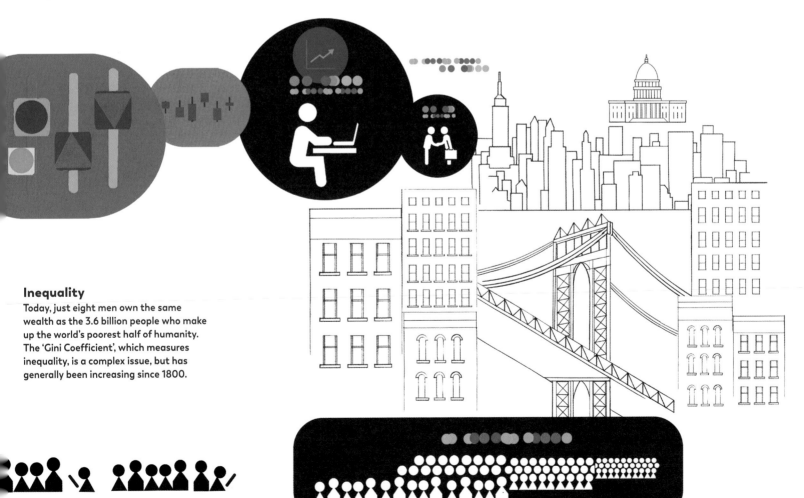

Out of control

Over the centuries, as we have seen throughout this book, humans have been able to extend our control of the natural world. More information has enabled us to manufacture better tools, which can then gather more and more resources. But now we are coming to a problem: the limits of our planet.

The need for change

Although there is an urgent need for us to live differently, we seem unable to change. Why is that? Our media system, the means by which we get our information, is almost entirely dependent on advertising, which depends on us consuming more. Given this, it would be very difficult, if not impossible, to make meaningful change without first transforming our media.

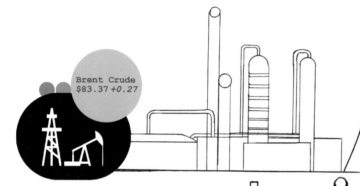

Brent Crude
$83.37 +0.27

Corporate media

Our media is driven by advertising. This means we recognize brand names and advertisements, but rarely see the conditions in which products are made. Factories and factory farms are almost entirely hidden from the public eye.

Economics is a major driver of human activity. But environmental damage is not factored enough into costs. Many companies have grown wealthy while damaging the environment.

$1.47

Humans and our livestock represent 96 percent of mammals on Earth. The remaining wild mammals, including every whale, bear, lion, or deer together, make up only 4 percent of the biomass of mammals on Earth.

260lb
$26.55

1.5 billion pigs are slaughtered each year.

The climate crisis

Although the science is clear, the world has not acted on the climate crisis. Every year since 1995, world leaders have met to try to reduce CO2 emissions. As of 2024, we have had more than 28 of these meetings, but after every single one, the CO2 has risen even more. Although most scientists are in agreement that climate change is humanity's greatest threat, there have still been no binding agreements. If our governments really cannot tackle this, are our democratic institutions fit for purpose?

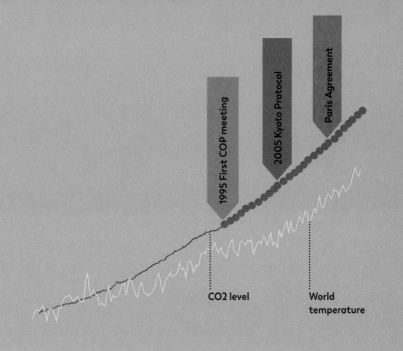

1995 First COP meeting

2005 Kyoto Protocol

Paris Agreement

CO2 level

World temperature

Deforestation

Annually we cut down around 15 billion trees globally, and plant 5 billion. That means we are losing about 10 billion trees a year. An area of forest the size of a soccer field disappears every second. Around 80 percent of this land is for animal agriculture.

69 percent of global wildlife has disappeared since 1970.

Information and imagination

Anthropologist David Graeber talks in his books about two opposing forces in society—the creative power of human imagination, and the corrupting forces of power. These forces can be seen at work throughout this book. Civilization, he argues, does not just happen; we make it happen. We imagine things we like and bring them into being. But something has gone wrong. Because who, if they could imagine any kind of world they liked, would imagine this one?

"The ultimate hidden truth of the world is that it is something that we make and could just as easily make differently".

—David Graeber

Another world is possible

Things can be different. Laws can be changed, copyright can be changed, privacy protections can be changed. All our laws were imagined, and so, can be reimagined. Reforms are being called for today by many leading thinkers. These changes may seem unimaginable, but all sorts of ideas like these once seemed unimaginable: democracy, abolition, voting rights for women. When these ideas were challenged, society changed. Let's take a closer look at how society changes.

Social change

From democracy, the abolition of slavery, and the rise of women's rights, civil rights, and queer rights, we have become used to the idea of society progressing and changing over time. But have you ever thought about why it changes? This is also down to information.

Predicting the future

Future predictions underestimate social change. In 1950, an article called *Miracles You'll See in the Next 50 Years* was published. Among the claims was "Housewives in 50 years may wash dirty dishes right down the drain—cheap plastic plates would melt in hot water." When we imagine the future we tend to imagine society as we know it but just with new technology. The author of this article never anticipated the word 'housewives' would soon be seen as outdated. He also seemed to lack any concern for the environment. What ideas in today's society will seem absurd in 70 years time?

Understanding the past

Martin Luther King Jr, Nelson Mandela, the suffragettes, and others are respected icons of history. However, in their time, some were branded as terrorists and their causes were seen by many as hopeless. Many were imprisoned, and some were killed. Just as we fail to understand how our society will change in future, we also sometimes forget how much society has changed already.

Ranters
Tree-huggers   Chartists
Levellers
                    Marx & Engels   IWW
        Abolitionists   Kropotkin   suffragettes
            May Day Strikes
                Rosa Luxemburg   Sylvia Pankhurst
                            Mahatma Gandhi   White Rose   Maya Angelou
                                Hannah Arendt   Malcolm X   James Baldwin
                                                                      Nelson Mandela
                                                                      Greenham Common
                                                                          May '68

Civil disobedience

Henry David Thoreau popularized the term 'Civil disobedience.' He refused to pay taxes because of his opposition to slavery and war. In Ireland, tenants decided to resist British rule by nonviolently refusing to pay landlords. Charles Boycott was the first to suffer this treatment. The protest was effective, and 'to boycott' became a verb. Mahatma Gandhi employed similar tactics to oppose British rule in India. He advocated holding no anger toward his opponents and to suffer their violent retaliations. Pictured on this page are just a sample of activists from over the past two centuries.

Emily Davison

Emily Davison was a suffragette who fought for votes for women in Britain. She was arrested nine times, and went on hunger strike seven times. She died after being hit by the King's horse when she walked onto a racetrack in protest.

Martin Luther King Jr.

The press branded civil rights campaigner Martin Luther King Jr. 'the most hated man in America.' False stories were spread about him, he was imprisoned 29 times, he and his family were spied on, his home was bombed, and he was attacked in the street. He stuck to his principles of nonviolence throughout. Although he was ultimately assassinated, many of his ideas have become mainstream. Today, he is admired throughout much of the world.

1800   1900   1950

Protest does work

Despite some setbacks, the world is overall becoming more democratic. The 'Polity scale' ranks countries on their democratic institutions on a scale of 0–10. In 1800, there would have been no countries that would have scored above an 8, but today there are 65. Many Nordic countries, Japan, Uruguay, and several others score 10/10, while the US and UK score 8/10. The US is defined as a 'flawed democracy' for a number of reasons, most notably because of the way it allows money to influence politics.

The Polity scale has been slowly climbing over the 19th and 20th centuries, and saw a steep increase in the second half of the 20th century. Overall, this is very positive.

Young people have played a very significant role in social change and protests all throughout history.

Books

Books play a major role in shaping society, which is why they have been banned or burned across history. Marx's *Das Kapital* is one of the most influential books on all time. *To Kill A Mockingbird*, and *The Feminine Mystique* led to huge shifts in thought about race and feminism in the 20th century. And the 1962 book *Silent Spring* helped form the environmental movement and brought a global ban on a pesticide used in farming.

Social change vs technological change

While pioneers of social change often suffer adversity and hardship in their lifetimes, technological pioneers are rewarded with enormous wealth. Today, Artificial Intelligence (AI) is seen as the next technology that will transform the world. Tech companies are putting huge funding into its development. A race has begun—a race for information itself. The more data an AI is fed, the better it will perform. The companies, or company, with the most data will be the ones that will dominate this next frontier.

Harvey Milk

Audre Lorde

Occupy Wall St

Anonymous

Wangari Maathai

Extinction Rebellion

Greta Thunberg

Marsha P. Johnson
An American gay liberation activist and drag queen, Johnson was one of the prominent figures in the Stonewall uprising of 1969. Like other members of the trans community, she was often violently attacked. She often claimed her middle name was 'Pay no mind.' She died in suspicious circumstances after she was seen being attacked by a mob.

Ken Saro-Wiwa
Nigerian poet and activist Ken Saro-Wiwa led a nonviolent campaign against the oil company that was polluting his homeland. He criticized the Nigerian military dictatorship for its reluctance to enforce environmental regulations. He and eight others were killed in 1995.

Wangari Maathai
Kenyan political activist Wangari Maathai was instrumental in the Kenyan Democracy movement. Fighting corruption, she faced arrests and physical attacks. Later, she founded an environmental organization focused on the planting of trees, conservation, and women's rights.

2000

Artificial Intelligence

In the 1950s, a group of computer scientists began to shift their focus. Rather than writing software to solve a problem, they would give the computer the tools to solve problems for itself. Computers were being taught to learn, to process language, and to identify objects. A term was coined to describe this new field: Artificial Intelligence.

Deep learning

Early Artificial Intelligence, or AI, was able to play chess and prove some mathematical theories, but progress was slow. In the 2000s, however, faster computers and big data helped speed up a process called 'deep learning.' Deep learning uses 'neural networks' to mimic the way the human brain learns. In 2012, it outperformed other forms of machine learning at image recognition. Since then, it is being applied to a wide range of applications.

Image recognition

Millions of images tagged with information are fed into neural networks. This trains the AI to recognize what is contained in the images. For example, one system was fed with scans tagged by trained cancer specialists. Soon, the AI was able to identify early cancer more accurately than doctors. In almost every area of visual recognition AI now outperforms humans.

Neural networks

Deep learning involves the use of neural networks with multiple layers. Each node, or point, on a network extracts a feature. Each layer along the network extracts higher-level features from the previous layer's output. In the image recognition network below there are five layers. When an image is fed into the network below, the first layer extracts edges from pixels, the next identifies parts from the edges, and the next recognizes objects from the parts. This hierarchy is key because it allows models to learn and identify very complex relationships within the data.

Training sets

The success of AI relies on the quantity of input data. One AI tool, Midjourney, used 100 million images for its training set. ChatGPT used 300 billion words. This is controversial because this data was used without permission.

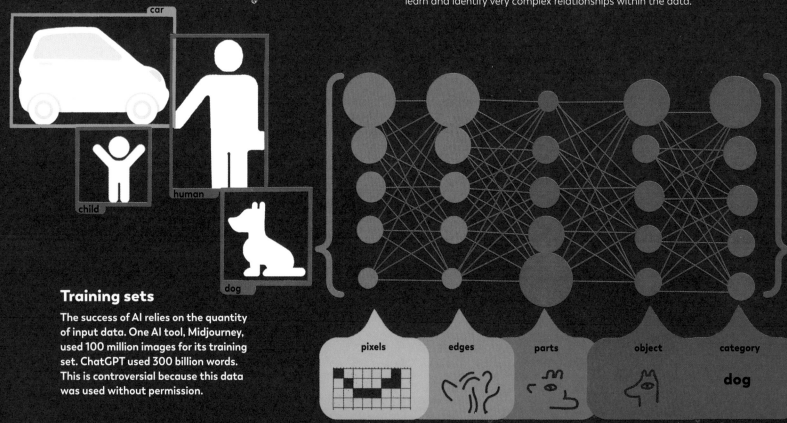

car

child

human

dog

pixels

edges

parts

object

category

dog

The AI revolution

Today's revolution in AI is predicted to have a similar effect on society as the Industrial Revolution did in the 1800s. During the Industrial Revolution, steam-powered machines began replacing manual workers. This caused a huge increase in productivity, and a surge in wealth for some, but as skilled workers were replaced by machines, mass unemployment led to mass exploitation. This in turn led to a backlash, and unions fought for the healthcare and welfare support we enjoy today. AI has the potential to change society in an even more dramatic way. Nearly half of all jobs today are predicted to become obsolete in the coming decades. How will we adapt to this?

The Singularity

The Singularity is the theory that at some point in the future, AI will become so advanced that it exceeds human intelligence and control. This could begin a 'runaway' technological acceleration with unknown consequences for society.

AI image generation

For AI to create an image, the image recognition process is reversed. A network trained to recognize dogs can be given a blank image and asked to try to recognize a dog. If there is nothing visible, the machine will make some marks and recognize areas of these that resemble features of a dog, such as pointed ears. It highlights and emphasizes those, and the process is repeated over and over until the computer 'draws' a dog from nothing.

Semantic networks

Another type of neural network, called a 'GPT,' works with text. ChatGPT launched in 2022 and became a sensation. AIs that are trained on language create webs of meaning called 'semantic networks' that allow them to figure out relationships between words. However, because they are trained on information added by humans, they reproduce and reinforce existing human biases. This is already causing problems today. AI is already being used to analyze credit ratings, mortgage approvals, job applications, and prison probations.

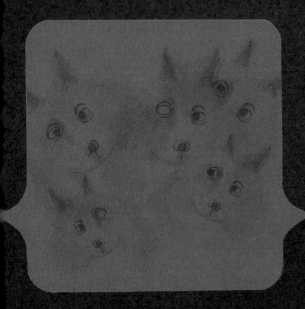

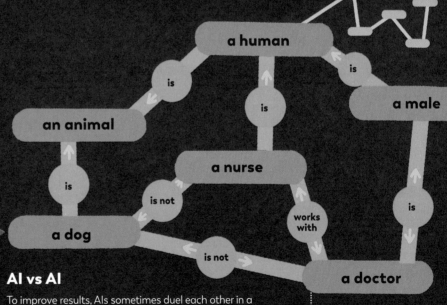

AI vs AI

To improve results, AIs sometimes duel each other in a process called adversarial training. To create realistic images, for example, a 'generator network' creates images while a 'discriminator network' tries to guess whether the image is real or fake. The two networks are trained together, which leads to the generation of highly realistic images.

From analyzing texts, biases are enforced. AIs have assumed nurses to be female and doctors to be male.

139

The mind

From language to drawing and print to computing, all the different media we have seen in this book are just different ways of conveying and processing information. In the end, however, it all comes back to us, and our minds. Information is nothing if it is not understood. But what is understanding?

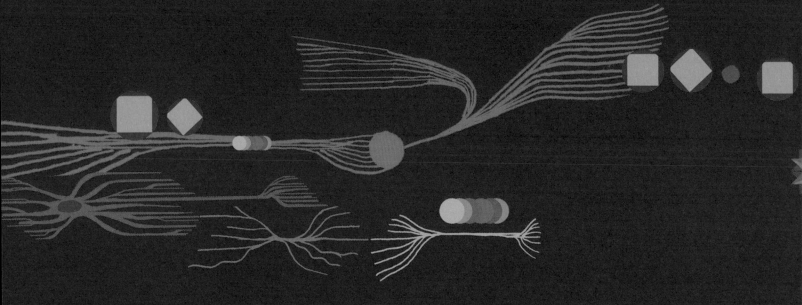

A human brain contains almost 100 billion neurons. Each of these tiny neurons can have up to 15,000 connections with other neurons, giving trillions of different possible combinations.

Understanding understanding

How do we understand? What is understanding? We have absolutely no idea. We know almost nothing about how our brains work. We know our minds interpret sensations to create our experiences, such as how we feel the warmth of the sun on our skin, or see the color of the sea with our eyes. These sensations are then turned into experiences by the brain. Our brain itself has never seen the outside world—it is encased in darkness inside our skulls. Yet somehow, it creates all we experience, our consciousness. In a very real sense it creates the world.

Other minds

The philosopher Thomas Nagel wrote a very influential paper in 1974 called *What Is It Like to Be a Bat?* In it, he describes the difficulty of understanding consciousness. Its subjective nature undermines any attempt to explain it with the usual scientific means. He explains this by asking us to imagine how it is to be a bat. While it may be possible to imagine what it might be like to fly, navigate by sonar, hang upside down, and eat insects like a bat, it cannot possibly be the same as experiencing the world through a bat's perspective.

The dreaming
Every culture has its own creation myths. Some cultures believe the world was made in six days. Others believe the creator god was hatched from a golden egg. Australian cultures are the only ones to believe the world was dreamed into being. The beforetime is sometimes referred to as 'the dreaming.' Perhaps there is a very real truth to this ancient belief.

Beyond death

Some technologists believe that in the future, we might find a way to transfer our conscious experience outside of our bodies. If so, our consciousness might transcend our bodies and maybe even transcend death. This is an idea called 'transhumanism.' Will we be able to build a machine that processes information just like we do? And if so, would it be conscious? And what if we could then enhance it? As information technology develops, it will continue to raise

Reality is not what it seems

We perceive the world. We see colors. But in a sense what we experience as color doesn't *really* exist in the real world. Each color is caused by a different frequency of light. But the actual experience of that color—its 'redness'—is really a perception. This perception, like all others, is created by the brain. Norbert Wiener wrote that "information is information, it is neither matter nor energy." Could it be possible that the world as we know it doesn't exist? There is no matter, no energy, no time and space? All there is...is information?

INDEX

> "The food of the woodpigeon is the miro berry, the forest is its world.
>
> The food of the people is knowledge, the world is their forest."
>
> —Maori saying

From the author:

The idea and materials for this book was inspired by a 2006 University of Berkeley, California course, The History of Information, created by Geoff Nunberg and Paul Duguid. Sadly, Geoff passed away in 2020. Paul very kindly helped consult on this book. I am hugely indebted to them both. I would also like to thank my agent, Debbie Bibo, Loonie Park for all her research, ideas, and writing. My editor, James Mitchem, art editor Charlotte Milner, and all the team at DK Books. David Cromwell and David Edwards of medialens.org, Daishu Ma, Moa Pårup, Nika Dubrovsky, Matt Taylor, Ed Vere, Mukul Patel, Jonathan Hulland, Richard Gizbert, and Gilad Lotan. The font was made by Andreas Pohancenik.

ACKNOWLEDGMENTS

The publisher would like to thank the following people for their generous assistance in the preparation of this book:

Sonia Charbonnier, William Collins, Stevie Crozier, Tom Morse, and Andreas Pohancenik for various DTP, font, and technical assistance. Martin Copeland, Nathalie Coupland, Nicola Evans, and Kirsty Howarth for their legal assistance and expertise. Justine Willis for proofreading. Marie Lorimer for indexing. Simon Mumford for cartography. Lisa Gillespie and Phil Ormerod for their insight and expertise. The entirety of the DK sales and marketing teams. And Fay Evans and Debbie Bibo for helping getting this project off the ground.

The publisher would like to thank the following for their kind permission to reproduce their photographs:
(Key: a-above; b-below/bottom; c-center; f-far; l-left; r-right; t-top)

AAM Archives Committee: AAM Archive, Bodleian Library 136 (15); **Alamy Stock Photo:** adsR 107cl, AF Fotografie 56cra, agefotostock / Historical Views 18c, Agefotostock / Tolo Balaguer 41cra (Grolier codex), Album 53cl, 77crb, 92crb (Mussolini), Alpha Stock 106clb, Art Collection 3 74clb (Illustrated London News), Associated Press / Anonymous 96clb, 97clb, Associated Press / Joseph R. Villarin 97cb, Associated Press / Richard Drew 95cl (Walter Cronkite), Neil Baylis 106cr, Book Worm 51tc, Sunny Celeste 48cl, Chronicle 38ca, 68c, 72cb, 77cra, 106crb, CPA Media Pte Ltd / Pictures From History 35cla, 60cl (Dog Head), CSU Archives / Everett Collection 136 (8), Darling Archive 57ca (Telescope), Design Pics Inc / Hawaiian Legacy Archive / Pacific Stock 93cb, Eraza Collection 67cl, Everett Collection Inc 37ca, 92crb (Coughlin), 94c, 94c (I Love Lucy), 94crb, 136 (12), Everett Collection, Inc. 91crb, f8 archive 106cb (PEPS ad), © Fine Art Images / Heritage Images 49ca, Florilegius 61cla, 61cla (Arterial system), 61ca, Gainew Gallery 57cr, Glasshouse Images / Circa Images 77c, 136 (4), Glasshouse Images / JT Vintage 71clb, GRANGER - Historical Picture Archive 44cb, 47tc, 47br, 67c, 67cr, 72clb, 73crb, 77ca, 78c, 105tl, 108clb (LUCKY STRIKE ad), 136 (1), Gibson Green 71clb (BurkeReflections), Patrick Guenette 70clb (stamp), Shim Harno 38cra, 77cb (Train), Hi-Story 103cl, Historic Collection 44cb (Chaobao), 68cr, Historic Images 59crb, 78c (Anne), 91cb, Historica Graphica Collection / Heritage Images 77clb, History and Art Collection 92ca, Hum Images 136 (7), IanDagnall Computing 79cb (Mickey Mouse), 102cra, 102c, imageBROKER / Logo Factory 79crb (Autoconf logo), 79crb (Linux Logo), INTERFOTO / History 79clb, 136 (10), INTERFOTO / Personalities 52bc, Jeff Speaks 53c, John Frost Newspapers 74clb (Manchester Guardian), 74cb (Daily Mail), Lanmas 18-19ca, Lebrecht Music & Arts / Lebrecht Authors 101cra, Lenscap 75cb, Logic Images 133tl, Lynden Pioneer Museum 93clb (Rinso), Magite Historic 59cb, Maidun Collection 136 (3), MAXPPP / Hanna

Franzn / TT 137cb, Patti McConville 107c, Moviestore Collection Ltd 77crb (Charlie Chaplin), Niday Picture Library 70clb, NMUIM 40cb, 41ca, Penta Springs Limited / Artokoloro 70cb, Penta Springs Limited / Corantos 72crb, Photo Vault 34cla, Pictorial Press Ltd 50ca, 56cb, 61ca (Encyclopedie), 76cb, 102cr, 107tl, Retro AdArchives 106c (Campbells), 108clb, Maurice Savage 74cl, 75clb, 136 (2), Science History Images / Photo Researchers 57ca, 69cr, Some Wonderful Old Things 84crb, Stockimo / Julesy 137ca (Act Now), Stocktrek Images / Vernon Lewis Gallery 102cl, Studioshots 83c, Sddeutsche Zeitung Photo / Scherl 76clb, Svintage Archive 70crb, Amoret Tanner 101cb, The History Collection 41cra, 60cra, 72cb (the great moon), The National Trust Photolibrary / John Hammond 69c (Interest-Book), The Natural History Museum 61tl, The Picture Art Collection 16c, 23cb, 52bl, 71cb, 78cb, The Print Collector / Ann Ronan Picture Library / Heritage-Images 78crb, The Print Collector / Heritage Images 39cla, The Print Collector / The Cartoon Collector / Heritage-Images / John Tenniel 101c, The Reading Room 16crb, 79tc, Thislife Pictures / Thislifethen 83cr, Universal Art Archive 52cr, 57cb, 57cl, 71clb (Rights of Man), Universal Images Group North America Llc / Marka / EPS 77cb, Volgi archive 44crb, 56-57cb, © Warner Bros / Courtesy Everett Collection 96c, Colin Waters 121cl, Bill Waterson 93crb, World History Archive 18cr, 37cra, 38cla, 41ca (The Madrid Codex), 53bc, 57c, 69cl, Zoompics 136 (5), ZUMA Press, Inc. 95clb; **Bridgeman Images:** British Library, London, UK 67tl, British Library, London, UK / Charles Darwin 83bc, Giancarlo Costa 60cl, English School 61ca (Definition of Oats), English School, (17th century) / English 78cl, PVDE 77cr (Mary Claire), © The Advertising Archives 106cb; **Courtesy of The Bank of England:** 69c; **Depositphotos Inc:** Morphart 44br; **Dreamstime.com:** Boggy 28crb, Dragosphotos 137ca (Go Vegan), Eugenebsov 137cla (Pride Flag), Hibrida13 85tl, Daniel Kaesler 121c, Jasbir Kaur 137ca (Just Stop Oil), Lawcain 64cb, Auncha Mee 136 (13), Minerva853 137ca (Black lives matter), Zeeshan Naveed 79cb, Patrimonio Designs Limited 137ca (Occupy Wall St), Channarong Pherngjanda 87tr, Ricochet69 136 (14), 137ca (Extinction), Sazori 105cla, Studio3321 23crb; **courtesy Folger Shakespeare Library:** 53cr; **Getty Images:** Archive Photos / Kean Collection 83cr (To My Beloved One), Archive Photos / The New York Historical Society 73clb (Yellow Kid), Bettmann 92crb (Hitler), 96crb, Hulton Archive / Fox Photos / Stringer 67c (Daily Courant), Hulton Archive / Print Collector 101crb, Michael Ochs Archives 93cb (Chuck Berry), Science & Society Picture Library 94clb, The Image Bank / Archive Holdings Inc. 95cl; **Getty Images / iStock:** DigitalVision Vectors / Whitemay 83cr (Victorian Christmas card), mj0007 70cb (We the People), Photos.com 53bc (Pepper Plant); **IEEE:** The Design of Colossus (foreword by Howard Campaigne) / Thomas H. Flowers 118c; **Library of Congress, Washington, D.C.:** 39ca, 76br, Keep America Beautiful 108crb, New York evening journal 73crb (Spain Guilty), New York journal and advertiser 73cb (New York

journal), 73cb (The Evening World.), Marion S Trikosko 136 (11), Wollstonecraft, Mary, Susan B Anthony, and Susan B. Anthony Collection 71tl, WPA Federal Art Project / Isadore Posoff, 108cb; **The Metropolitan Museum of Art:** H.O. Havemeyer Collection, Gift of Horace Havemeyer, 1929 36cl; **Museum of American Finance:** 85cb; **NASA:** 96cb; **Paris Museums:** Carnavalet Museum, History of Paris / Imprimerie Valle 70cr; **Rare Books and Special Collections, University of Sydney Library:** 57cra; **Science Photo Library:** 42br, Middle Temple Library 54bc; **Scientific Research Publishing Inc.:** The History of the Derivation of Eulers Number / Mohsen Aghaeiboorkheili & John Giuna Kawagle 56c; **Shutterstock.com:** 360b 105ca (OBERSALZBERG), Scott Cornell 103c, Everett Collection 73cb, 105ca, 105cr, 136 (6), Siam Vector 136 (9), Kharbine-Tapabor 77cr, Universal / Kobal 103cr, windmoon 35tl, Anastasiia Zhadan 137cla (Love is not a Crime); **SuperStock:** Science and Society / SM / SSPL 116-117b; © **Telegraph Media Group Limited:** 74clb (Telegraph); © **The Sainsbury Archive:** 106c (J. Sainsbury); **Wellcome Collection:** 58crb, 59clb, 59cb (Natural and political observations), 61cra

Data Credits

WORLDPOPULATIONHISTORY.ORG: Based on map and dataset compilation by Population Education (populationeducation.org) / (worldpopulationhistory. org) 6t, 16t, 28t, 42t, 54t, 64t, 80t, 88t, 98t, 112t

All other images © Dorling Kindersley Limited.